ISEE®

Skill Practice

Independent School Entrance Exam Practice Test Questions

Published by
Complete TEST Preparation Inc.

Copyright © 2013 by Complete Test Preparation Inc. ALL RIGHTS RESERVED. No part of this book may be reproduced or transferred in any form or by any means, graphic, electronic, or mechanical, including photocopying, recording, web distribution, taping, or by any information storage retrieval system, without the written permission of the author.

Notice: Complete Test Preparation Inc. makes every reasonable effort to obtain from reliable sources accurate, complete, and timely information about the tests covered in this book. Nevertheless, changes can be made in the tests or the administration of the tests at any time and Complete Test Preparation Inc. makes no representation or warranty, either expressed or implied as to the accuracy, timeliness, or completeness of the information contained in this book. Complete Test Preparation Inc. makes no representations or warranties of any kind, express or implied, about the completeness, accuracy, reliability, suitability or availability with respect to the information contained in this document for any purpose. Any reliance you place on such information is therefore strictly at your own risk.

The author(s) shall not be liable for any loss incurred as a consequence of the use and application, directly or indirectly, of any information presented in this work. Sold with the understanding, the author(s) is not engaged in rendering professional services or advice. If advice or expert assistance is required, the services of a competent professional should be sought.

The company, product and service names used in this publication are for identification purposes only. All trademarks and registered trademarks are the property of their respective owners. Complete Test Preparation Inc. is not affiliated with any educational institution.

ISEE® and the Independent School Entrance Exam are registered trademarks of Educational Records Bureau, who are not involved in the production of, and do not endorse this publication.

We strongly recommend that students check with exam providers for up-to-date information regarding test content.

Published by
Complete Test Preparation Inc.
Victoria BC Canada
Visit us on the web at http://www.test-preparation.ca
Printed in the USA

About Complete Test Preparation Inc.

Complete Test Preparation Inc. has been publishing high quality study materials since 2005. Thousands of students visit our websites every year, and thousands of students, teachers and parents all over the world have purchased our teaching materials, curriculum, study guides and practice tests.

Complete Test Preparation Inc. is committed to providing students with the best study materials and practice tests available on the market. Members of our team combine years of teaching experience, with experienced writers and editors, all with advanced degrees.

ISBN-13: 9781772450965

Version 6.6 October 2015

Contents

6 **Getting Started**
How this study guide is organized 7
The ISEE® Study Plan 8
Making a Study Schedule 8

14 **Practice Test Questions Set 1**
Answer Key 73

95 **Practice Test Questions Set 2**
Answer Key 154

176 **Conclusion**

177 **Multiple Choice Secrets Special Offer**

Getting Started

CONGRATULATIONS! By deciding to take the Independent School Entrance Exam (ISEE®), you have taken the first step toward a great future! Of course, there is no point in taking this important examination unless you intend to do your very best to earn the highest grade you possibly can. That means getting yourself organized and discovering the best approaches, methods and strategies to master the material. Yes, that will require real effort and dedication on your part but if you are willing to focus your energy and devote the study time necessary, before you know it you will be on you way to a brighter future!

We know that taking on a new endeavour can be a little scary, and it is easy to feel unsure of where to begin. That's where we come in. This study guide is designed to help you improve your test-taking skills, show you a few tricks of the trade and increase both your competency and confidence.

The Independent School Entrance Exam

The ISEE® exam is composed of five sections, verbal reasoning, quantitative skills, reading, mathematics and language skills. The verbal reasoning section consists of analogies, synonyms and antonyms, logic and verbal classification. The quantitative skills section consists of number series, geometric and non geometric comparisons, and basic math. The reading section consists of reading comprehension and vocabulary questions. The mathematics section consists of problem solving questions or word problems. The language skills section consists of punctuation and capitalization, English usage, spelling and composition.

While we seek to make our guide as comprehensive as possible, note that like all exams, the ISEE® Exam might be adjusted at some future point. New material might be added, or content that is no longer relevant or applicable might be removed. It is always a good idea to give the materials you receive when you register to take the ISEE® a careful review.

The ISEE® Study Plan

Now that you have made the decision to take the ISEE®, it is time to get started. Before you do another thing, you will need to figure out a plan of attack. The very best study tip is to start early! The longer the time period you devote to regular study practice, the more likely you will be to retain the material and be able to access it quickly. If you thought that 1x20 is the same as 2x10, guess what? It really is not, when it comes to study time. Reviewing material for just an hour per day over the course of 20 days is far better than studying for two hours a day for only 10 days. The more often you revisit a particular piece of information, the better you will know it. Not only will your grasp and understanding be better, but your ability to reach into your brain and quickly and efficiently pull out the tidbit you need, will be greatly enhanced as well.

The great Chinese scholar and philosopher Confucius believed that true knowledge could be defined as knowing both what you know and what you do not know. The first step in preparing for the ISEE® is to assess your strengths and weaknesses. You may already have an idea of what you know and what you do not know, but evaluating yourself using our Self- Assessment modules for each of the three areas, Math, Writing and Quantitative skills, will clarify the details.

Making a Study Schedule

To make your study time most productive, you will need to develop a study plan. The purpose of the plan is to organize all the bits of pieces of information in such a way that you will not feel overwhelmed. Rome was not built in a day, and learning everything you will need to know to pass the ISEE® is going to take time, too. Arranging the material you need to learn into manageable chunks is the best way to go. Each study session should make you feel as though you have succeeded in accomplishing your goal, and your goal is simply to learn what you planned to learn during that particular session. Try to organize the content in such a way that each study session builds upon previous ones. That way, you will retain the information, be better able to access it, and review the previous bits and pieces at the same time.

Self-assessment

The Best Study Tip! The very best study tip is to start early! The longer you study regularly, the more you will retain and 'learn' the material. Studying for 1 hour per day for 20 days is far better than studying for 2 hours for 10 days.

What don't you know?

The first step is to assess your strengths and weaknesses. You may already have an idea of where your weaknesses are, or you can take our Self-assessment modules for each of the content areas.

Exam Component	Rate 1 to 5
Verbal Reasoning	
Synonyms	
Sentence Completion	
Quantitative Reasoning	

Problem Solving	
Quantitative Comparison	
Mathematics	
Arithmetic	
Algebra	
Geometry	
Reading Comprehension	

Making a Study Schedule

The key to making a study plan is to divide the material you need to learn into manageable sized pieces and learn it, while at the same time reviewing the material that you already know.

Using the table above, any scores of 3 or below, you need to spend time learning, going over and practicing this subject area. A score of 4 means you need to review the material, but you don't have to spend time re-learning. A score of 5 and you are OK with just an occasional review before the exam.

A score of 0 or 1 means you really need to work on this should allocate the most time and the highest priority. Some students prefer a 5-day plan and others a 10-day plan. It also depends on how much time you have until the exam.

Here is an example of a 5-day plan based on an example from the table above:

Synonyms: 1- Study 1 hour everyday – review on last day

Quantitative Comparisons: 3 - Study 1 hour for 3 days then ½ hour a day, then review
Problem Solving (Word Problems): 4 - Review every second day
Geometric Comparison: 2 - Study 1 hour first day then ½ hour everyday

Algebra: 5 - Review for ½ hour every other day
Reading Comp.: 5 - Review for ½ hour every other day

Using this example, reading comprehension and algebra are good and only need occasional review. Geometric Comparison is good and needs 'some' review. Quantitative Comparisons needs a bit of work, Word Problems need a lot of work and Synonyms are very weak and need the most time. Based on this, here is a sample study plan:

Day	Subject	Time
Monday		
Study	Synonyms	1 hour
Study	Word Problems	1 hour
½ **hour break**		
Study	Quantitative Comparisons	1 hour
Review	Reading Comp.	½ hour
Tuesday		
Study	Synonyms	1 hour
Study	Word Problems	½ hour
½ **hour break**		
Study	Quantitative Comparisons	½ hour
Review	Algebra	½ hour
Review	Reading Comp.	½ hour
Wednesday		
Study	Synonyms	1 hour
Study	Word Problems	½ hour
½ **hour break**		
Study	Quantitative Comparisons	½ hour
Review	Reading Comp.	½ hour
Thursday		
Study	Synonyms	½ hour
Study	Word Problems	½ hour
Review	Quantitative Comparisons	½ hour
½ **hour break**		
Review	Reading Comp.	½ hour
Review	Algebra	½ hour
Friday		
Review	Synonyms	½ hour
Review	Word Problems	½ hour
Review	Quantitative Comparisons	½ hour
½ **hour break**		
Review	Algebra	½ hour
Review	Reading Comp.	½ hour

Using this example, adapt the study plan to your own schedule. This schedule assumes 2 ½ - 3 hours available to study everyday for a 5 day period.

First, write out what you need to study and how much. Next figure out how many days you have before the test. Note, do NOT study on the last day before the test. On the last day before the test, you won't learn anything and will probably only confuse yourself.

Make a table with the days before the test and the number of hours you have available to study each day. We suggest working with 1 hour and ½ hour time slots.

Start filling in the blanks, with the subjects you need to study the most getting the most time and the most regular time slots (i.e. everyday) and the subjects that you know getting the least time (e.g. ½ hour every other day, or every 3rd day).

Tips for making a schedule

Once you make a schedule, stick with it! Make your study sessions reasonable. If you make a study schedule and don't stick with it, you set yourself up for failure. Instead, schedule study sessions that are a bit shorter and set yourself up for success! Make sure your study sessions are do-able. Studying is hard work but after you pass, you can party and take a break!

Schedule breaks. Breaks are just as important as study time. Work out a rotation of studying and breaks that works for you.

Build up study time. If you find it hard to sit still and study for 1 hour straight through, build up to it. Start with 20 minutes, and then take a break. Once you get used to 20-minute study sessions, increase the time to 30 minutes. Gradually work you way up to 1 hour.

40 minutes to 1 hour is optimal. Studying for longer than this is tiring and not productive. Studying for shorter isn't long enough to be productive.

Studying Math. Studying Math is different from studying other subjects because you use a different part of your brain. The best way to study math is to practice everyday. This will train your mind to think in a mathematical way. If you miss a day or days, the mathematical mind-set is gone and you have to start all over again to build it up.

Study and practice math everyday for at least 5 days before the exam.

For more information, see our How to Study Guide at www.study-skills.ca.

Practice Test Questions Set 1

THE QUESTIONS BELOW ARE NOT THE SAME AS YOU WILL FIND ON THE ISEE® - THAT WOULD BE TOO EASY! And nobody knows what the questions will be and they change all the time. Below are general questions that cover the same subject areas as the ISEE®. So, while the format and exact wording of the questions may differ slightly, and change from year to year, if you can answer the questions below, you will have no problem with the ISEE®.

For the best results, take these practice test questions as if it were the real exam. Set aside time when you will not be disturbed, and a location that is quiet and free of distractions. Read the instructions carefully, read each question carefully, and answer to the best of your ability.

Use the bubble answer sheets provided. When you have completed the practice questions, check your answer against the Answer Key and read the explanation provided.

Do not attempt more than one set of practice test questions in one day. After completing the first practice test, wait two or three days before attempting the second set of questions.

Section I – Verbal Reasoning
Questions: 40
Time: 20 Minutes

Section II – Quantitative Reasoning
Questions: 35
Time: 35 Minutes

Section III – Reading Comprehension
Questions: 40
Time: 40 Minutes

Section IV – Mathematics
Questions: 45
Time: 40 Minutes

Verbal Reasoning

1. A B C D
2. A B C D
3. A B C D
4. A B C D
5. A B C D
6. A B C D
7. A B C D
8. A B C D
9. A B C D
10. A B C D
11. A B C D
12. A B C D
13. A B C D
14. A B C D
15. A B C D
16. A B C D
17. A B C D
18. A B C D
19. A B C D
20. A B C D
21. A B C D
22. A B C D
23. A B C D
24. A B C D
25. A B C D
26. A B C D
27. A B C D
28. A B C D
29. A B C D
30. A B C D
31. A B C D
32. A B C D
33. A B C D
34. A B C D
35. A B C D
36. A B C D
37. A B C D
38. A B C D
39. A B C D
40. A B C D

Quantitative Reasoning

1. Ⓐ Ⓑ Ⓒ Ⓓ   18. Ⓐ Ⓑ Ⓒ Ⓓ
2. Ⓐ Ⓑ Ⓒ Ⓓ   19. Ⓐ Ⓑ Ⓒ Ⓓ
3. Ⓐ Ⓑ Ⓒ Ⓓ   20. Ⓐ Ⓑ Ⓒ Ⓓ
4. Ⓐ Ⓑ Ⓒ Ⓓ   21. Ⓐ Ⓑ Ⓒ Ⓓ
5. Ⓐ Ⓑ Ⓒ Ⓓ   22. Ⓐ Ⓑ Ⓒ Ⓓ
6. Ⓐ Ⓑ Ⓒ Ⓓ   23. Ⓐ Ⓑ Ⓒ Ⓓ
7. Ⓐ Ⓑ Ⓒ Ⓓ   24. Ⓐ Ⓑ Ⓒ Ⓓ
8. Ⓐ Ⓑ Ⓒ Ⓓ   25. Ⓐ Ⓑ Ⓒ Ⓓ
9. Ⓐ Ⓑ Ⓒ Ⓓ   26. Ⓐ Ⓑ Ⓒ Ⓓ
10. Ⓐ Ⓑ Ⓒ Ⓓ   27. Ⓐ Ⓑ Ⓒ Ⓓ
11. Ⓐ Ⓑ Ⓒ Ⓓ   28. Ⓐ Ⓑ Ⓒ Ⓓ
12. Ⓐ Ⓑ Ⓒ Ⓓ   29. Ⓐ Ⓑ Ⓒ Ⓓ
13. Ⓐ Ⓑ Ⓒ Ⓓ   30. Ⓐ Ⓑ Ⓒ Ⓓ
14. Ⓐ Ⓑ Ⓒ Ⓓ   31. Ⓐ Ⓑ Ⓒ Ⓓ
15. Ⓐ Ⓑ Ⓒ Ⓓ   32. Ⓐ Ⓑ Ⓒ Ⓓ
16. Ⓐ Ⓑ Ⓒ Ⓓ   33. Ⓐ Ⓑ Ⓒ Ⓓ
17. Ⓐ Ⓑ Ⓒ Ⓓ   34. Ⓐ Ⓑ Ⓒ Ⓓ
                35. Ⓐ Ⓑ Ⓒ Ⓓ

Reading Comprehension

1. Ⓐ Ⓑ Ⓒ Ⓓ   21. Ⓐ Ⓑ Ⓒ Ⓓ
2. Ⓐ Ⓑ Ⓒ Ⓓ   22. Ⓐ Ⓑ Ⓒ Ⓓ
3. Ⓐ Ⓑ Ⓒ Ⓓ   23. Ⓐ Ⓑ Ⓒ Ⓓ
4. Ⓐ Ⓑ Ⓒ Ⓓ   24. Ⓐ Ⓑ Ⓒ Ⓓ
5. Ⓐ Ⓑ Ⓒ Ⓓ   25. Ⓐ Ⓑ Ⓒ Ⓓ
6. Ⓐ Ⓑ Ⓒ Ⓓ   26. Ⓐ Ⓑ Ⓒ Ⓓ
7. Ⓐ Ⓑ Ⓒ Ⓓ   27. Ⓐ Ⓑ Ⓒ Ⓓ
8. Ⓐ Ⓑ Ⓒ Ⓓ   28. Ⓐ Ⓑ Ⓒ Ⓓ
9. Ⓐ Ⓑ Ⓒ Ⓓ   29. Ⓐ Ⓑ Ⓒ Ⓓ
10. Ⓐ Ⓑ Ⓒ Ⓓ   30. Ⓐ Ⓑ Ⓒ Ⓓ
11. Ⓐ Ⓑ Ⓒ Ⓓ   31. Ⓐ Ⓑ Ⓒ Ⓓ
12. Ⓐ Ⓑ Ⓒ Ⓓ   32. Ⓐ Ⓑ Ⓒ Ⓓ
13. Ⓐ Ⓑ Ⓒ Ⓓ   33. Ⓐ Ⓑ Ⓒ Ⓓ
14. Ⓐ Ⓑ Ⓒ Ⓓ   34. Ⓐ Ⓑ Ⓒ Ⓓ
15. Ⓐ Ⓑ Ⓒ Ⓓ   35. Ⓐ Ⓑ Ⓒ Ⓓ
16. Ⓐ Ⓑ Ⓒ Ⓓ   36. Ⓐ Ⓑ Ⓒ Ⓓ
17. Ⓐ Ⓑ Ⓒ Ⓓ   37. Ⓐ Ⓑ Ⓒ Ⓓ
18. Ⓐ Ⓑ Ⓒ Ⓓ   38. Ⓐ Ⓑ Ⓒ Ⓓ
19. Ⓐ Ⓑ Ⓒ Ⓓ   39. Ⓐ Ⓑ Ⓒ Ⓓ
20. Ⓐ Ⓑ Ⓒ Ⓓ   40. Ⓐ Ⓑ Ⓒ Ⓓ

Mathematics

1. Ⓐ Ⓑ Ⓒ Ⓓ
2. Ⓐ Ⓑ Ⓒ Ⓓ
3. Ⓐ Ⓑ Ⓒ Ⓓ
4. Ⓐ Ⓑ Ⓒ Ⓓ
5. Ⓐ Ⓑ Ⓒ Ⓓ
6. Ⓐ Ⓑ Ⓒ Ⓓ
7. Ⓐ Ⓑ Ⓒ Ⓓ
8. Ⓐ Ⓑ Ⓒ Ⓓ
9. Ⓐ Ⓑ Ⓒ Ⓓ
10. Ⓐ Ⓑ Ⓒ Ⓓ
11. Ⓐ Ⓑ Ⓒ Ⓓ
12. Ⓐ Ⓑ Ⓒ Ⓓ
13. Ⓐ Ⓑ Ⓒ Ⓓ
14. Ⓐ Ⓑ Ⓒ Ⓓ
15. Ⓐ Ⓑ Ⓒ Ⓓ
16. Ⓐ Ⓑ Ⓒ Ⓓ
17. Ⓐ Ⓑ Ⓒ Ⓓ
18. Ⓐ Ⓑ Ⓒ Ⓓ
19. Ⓐ Ⓑ Ⓒ Ⓓ
20. Ⓐ Ⓑ Ⓒ Ⓓ
21. Ⓐ Ⓑ Ⓒ Ⓓ
22. Ⓐ Ⓑ Ⓒ Ⓓ
23. Ⓐ Ⓑ Ⓒ Ⓓ
24. Ⓐ Ⓑ Ⓒ Ⓓ
25. Ⓐ Ⓑ Ⓒ Ⓓ
26. Ⓐ Ⓑ Ⓒ Ⓓ
27. Ⓐ Ⓑ Ⓒ Ⓓ
28. Ⓐ Ⓑ Ⓒ Ⓓ
29. Ⓐ Ⓑ Ⓒ Ⓓ
30. Ⓐ Ⓑ Ⓒ Ⓓ
31. Ⓐ Ⓑ Ⓒ Ⓓ
32. Ⓐ Ⓑ Ⓒ Ⓓ
33. Ⓐ Ⓑ Ⓒ Ⓓ
34. Ⓐ Ⓑ Ⓒ Ⓓ
35. Ⓐ Ⓑ Ⓒ Ⓓ
36. Ⓐ Ⓑ Ⓒ Ⓓ
37. Ⓐ Ⓑ Ⓒ Ⓓ
38. Ⓐ Ⓑ Ⓒ Ⓓ
39. Ⓐ Ⓑ Ⓒ Ⓓ
40. Ⓐ Ⓑ Ⓒ Ⓓ
41. Ⓐ Ⓑ Ⓒ Ⓓ
42. Ⓐ Ⓑ Ⓒ Ⓓ
43. Ⓐ Ⓑ Ⓒ Ⓓ
44. Ⓐ Ⓑ Ⓒ Ⓓ
45. Ⓐ Ⓑ Ⓒ Ⓓ

Part I – Synonyms

Directions: Choose the word that is closest in meaning to the given word.

1. **PECULIAR**
    a. New
    b. Strange
    c. Imaginative
    d. Funny

2. **TIPPET**
    a. Necktie
    b. Shawl
    c. Sweater
    d. Blouse

3. **VIVID**
    a. Glamorous
    b. Bountiful
    c. Varied
    d. Brilliant

4. **SEMBLANCE**
    a. Personality
    b. Image
    c. Attitude
    d. ambition

5. IMPREGNABLE

   a. Unconquerable

   b. Impossible

   c. Unlimited

   d. Imperfect

6. JARGON

   a. Slang

   b. Slander

   c. Plagiarism

   d. Outdated

7. RENDER

   a. Give

   b. Recognize

   c. Stem

   d. Adjust

8. INTRUSIVE

   a. Private

   b. Invasive

   c. Mysterious

   d. Unique

9. RENOWN

   a. Popular

   b. Safe

   c. Shy

   d. Curtail

10. INCOHERENT

  a. Ambiguous
  b. Lighthearted
  c. Jumbled
  d. Malignant

11. CONGENIAL

  a. Pleasant
  b. Distort
  c. Valuable
  d. Liability

12. PLIGHT

  a. Circumstance
  b. Scheme
  c. Whimsical
  d. Situation

13. BERATE

  a. Criticize
  b. Unspoken
  c. Tenet
  d. Turf

14. CONSTRUE

  a. Decide
  b. Design
  c. Interpret
  d. Examine

15. SCARED

    a. Surprised

    b. Grateful

    c. Happy

    d. Terrified

16. DEMONSTRATED

    a. Presented

    b. Exclaimed

    c. Handled

    d. Lectured

17. HALT

    a. Continue

    b. Start

    c. Stop

    d. Danger

18. STRANGE

    a. Popular

    b. Ordinary

    c. Unfamiliar

    d. Common

19. SEIZE

    a. Lose

    b. Choose

    c. Rob

    d. Win

20. DIVULGE

    a. Repeat

    b. Tell

    c. Write

    d. Imagine

Part II - Sentence Completion

Directions: For each sentence below, choose the word that best completes the sentence.

21. Through the use of powerful fans that circulate the heat over the food, _____ ovens work very efficiently.

    a. Microwave

    b. Broiler

    c. Convection

    d. Pressure

22. Because of the growing use of _____ as a fuel, corn production has greatly increased.

    a. Alcohol

    b. Ethanol

    c. Natural gas

    d. Oil

23. In heavily industrialized areas, the air pollution causes many _____ diseases.

    a. Respiratory

    b. Cardiac

    c. Alimentary

    d. Circulatory

24. Because hydroelectric power is a _____ source of energy, its use is considered a green energy.

    a. Significant

    b. Disposable

    c. Renewable

    d. Recyclable

25. The process required the use of highly _____ liquids, so fire extinguishers were everywhere in the factory.

    a. Erratic

    b. Combustible

    c. Inflammable

    d. Neutral

26. I still don't know exactly. That isn't _____ evidence.

    a. Undeterred

    b. Unrelenting

    c. Unfortunate

    d. Conclusive

27. He could manipulate the coins in his fingers very _____.

    a. Brazenly

    b. Eloquently

    c. Boisterously

    d. Deftly

28. His investment scheme _____ many serious investors, who lost money.

    a. Helped
    b. Vindicated
    c. Duped
    d. Reproved

29. When we go to a party, we always _____ a driver.

    a. Feign
    b. Exploit
    c. Dote
    d. Designate

30. This new evidence should _____ any doubts.

    a. Dispel
    b. Dispense
    c. Evaluate
    d. Diverse

31. She went to Asia on $10 a day – her _____ travelling plans are amazing.

    a. Frothy
    b. Frugal
    c. Fraught
    d. Focal

32. My grandmother's house is full or trinkets and ornaments. She is always buying _____.

  a. Collectibles
  b. Baubles
  c. China
  d. Crystal

33. I am finally out of debt! I paid off all of my _____.

  a. Debtors
  b. Defendants
  c. Accounts Receivable
  d. Creditors

34. I love listening to his speeches. He has a gift for _____.

  a. Oratory
  b. Irony
  c. Jargon
  d. None of the above

35. The warehouse went bankrupt so all the furniture has to be _____.

  a. Dissected
  b. Liquidated
  c. Destroyed
  d. Bought

36. He sold the property when he didn't even own it. The whole thing was a _____.

   a. Hoax
   b. Feign
   c. Defile
   d. Default

37. The repair really isn't working. Those parts you replaced are _____.

   a. Despondent
   b. Illusive
   c. Defective'
   d. Granular

38. Just because she is supervisor, doesn't mean we have to _____ in front of her.

   a. Foible
   b. Grovel
   c. Humiliate
   d. Indispose

39. That noise is _____ ! It is driving me crazy.

   a. Loud
   b. Intolerable
   c. Frivolous
   d. Fictitious

40. Her inheritance was a good size and included many _____.

  a. Heirlooms
  b. Perchance
  c. Cynical
  d. Lateral

Section II – Quantitative Reasoning

1. Solve for x. 5x + 21 = 66.

  a. 19
  b. 9
  c. 15
  d. 5

2. What is the least common multiple of 9 and 3?

  a. 27
  b. 9
  c. 3
  d. 18

3. How much water can be stored in a cylindrical container 5 meters in diameter and 12 meters high?

  a. 235.65 m^3
  b. 223.65 m^3
  c. 240.65 m^3
  d. 252.65 m^3

4. Estimate 215 x 65.

    a. 1,350
    b. 13,500
    c. 103,500
    d. 3,500

5. Richard gives 's' amount of salary to each of his 'n' employees weekly. If he has 'x' amount of money then how many days he can employ these 'n' employees.

    a. sx/7n
    b. 7x
    c. nx/7x
    d. 7x/ns

6. Below is the attendance for a class of 45.

Day	Absent Students
Monday	5
Tuesday	9
Wednesday	4
Thursday	10
Friday	6

What is the average attendance for the week?

    a. 88%
    b. 85%
    c. 81%
    d. 77%

7. A driver at a speed of 's' miles per hour can reach his destination in 'h' hours. If his speed increased from 's' to 'x' then how much less time in hours will it take to reach his destination?

    a. h – xh/s
    b. h - sh/x
    c. s/x
    d. sh/x

8. Write 41.061 to the nearest 10th.

    a. 41.1
    b. 41.06
    c. 41
    d. 41.6

9. Brad has agreed to buy everyone a Coke. Each drink costs $1.89, and there are 5 friends. Estimate Brad's cost.

    a. $7
    b. $8
    c. $10
    d. $12

10. In a train one morning, 24 people are sitting while 8 people are standing. What is the ratio of people sitting to standing?

    a. 1:3
    b. 1:5
    c. 3:1
    d. 3:5

11. Estimate 4,210,987 − 210,078

a. 4,000,000
b. 40, 000,000
c. 400,000
d. 40,000

12. $2^3 =$

a. 1/0.125
b. $\sqrt{16}$
c. 3^2
d. 5

13. 10^4 is not equal to which of the following?

a. 100,000
b. 0.1×10^5
c. 10 x 10 x 10 x 10
d. $10^2 \times 10^2$

14. Divide x^5 by x^2

a. x^7
b. x^4
c. x^{10}
d. x^3

15. Which of the following is not a fraction equivalent to 3/4?

a. 6/8
b. 9/12
c. 12/18
d. 21/28

16. Which of the following numbers is the greatest?

    a. 1
    b. √2
    c. 3/2
    d. 4/3

17. What number divided by 5 is 1/4 of 100?

    a. 125
    b. 150
    c. 75
    d. 225

Part II

Directions: Examine the quantities given in Column A and Column B of the table and choose the best answer.

18.

Column A	Column B
20 - X	X^2

$3X + 3 = 15$

    a. Column A is greater
    b. Column B is greater
    c. The quantities are equal
    d. The relationship cannot be determined

19.

Column A	Column B
2X + Y	2Y + X

X > 0, Y > 0

    a. Column A is greater
    b. Column B is greater
    c. The quantities are equal
    d. The relationship cannot be determined

20.

Column A	Column B
3	Y

$y^2 + 6 = 15$

    a. Column A is greater
    b. Column B is greater
    c. The quantities are equal
    d. The relationship cannot be determined

21.

Column A	Column B
A	14

2ab + 5 = 25

    a. Column A is greater
    b. Column B is greater
    c. The quantities are equal
    d. The relationship cannot be determined

22.

Column A	Column B
1/2	0.589/.35

    a. Column A is greater

    b. Column B is greater

    c. The quantities are equal

    d. The relationship cannot be determined

23.

Column A	Column B
2/3	0.589/.35

    a. Column A is greater

    b. Column B is greater

    c. The quantities are equal

    d. The relationship cannot be determined

24.

Column A	Column B
4/9 + 3/4	24/27

    a. Column A is greater

    b. Column B is greater

    c. The quantities are equal

    d. The relationship cannot be determined

25.

Column A	Column B
Susan's Savings	$75

Susan bought a dishwasher on sale for 20% off. She has a membership that gives her an additional 2% off the sale price. The full retail price of the dishwasher was $250.

    a. Column A is greater
    b. Column B is greater
    c. The quantities are equal
    d. The relationship cannot be determined

26.

Column A	Column B
3.1 hours	X hours

A car drove 135 km. at a speed of 50 km. per hour. Let X equal the time it took.

    a. Column A is greater
    b. Column B is greater
    c. The quantities are equal
    d. The relationship cannot be determined

27.

Column A	Column B
X pages	40 pages

A typist can type a full page in 2 minutes. Let X be the number of pages he can type in 1 hour.

    a. Column A is greater
    b. Column B is greater
    c. The quantities are equal
    d. The relationship cannot be determined

28.

Column A	Column B
X	$10.15

Jack bought 2 cheeseburgers for $3.00 each, a large fries for $1.99 and a Coke for $1.58. A tax of 3.2% was added. If he paid with a $20 bill, let X be the amount of change he received.

    a. Column A is greater
    b. Column B is greater
    c. The quantities are equal
    d. The relationship cannot be determined

29.

Column A	Column B
X	$645,730

A business owner has assets as follows:

Building: $580,000
Machinery: $255,000
Cash: $10,000

At the end of one year, the building has increased by 5.6%, the machinery has depreciated by 15% and he has $4500 in additional cash.

    a. Column A is greater
    b. Column B is greater
    c. The quantities are equal
    d. The relationship cannot be determined

30.

Column A	Column B
X	$40

Britney invested $500 in a fixed-term deposit for 2 years. Interest of 4% was paid yearly. Let X be the amount of interest she earned.

    a. Column A is greater
    b. Column B is greater
    c. The quantities are equal
    d. The relationship cannot be determined

31.

Column A	Column B
Average number of students absent	4

Below is the number of students absent for 1 week.

Monday: 5
Tuesday 8
Wednesday 2
Thursday 0
Friday 4

    a. Column A is greater

    b. Column B is greater

    c. The quantities are equal

    d. The relationship cannot be determined

32.

Column A	Column B
3/4 expressed as percent	80%

    a. Column A is greater

    b. Column B is greater

    c. The quantities are equal

    d. The relationship cannot be determined

33.

Column A	Column B
.78 as a fraction	8/10

    a. Column A is greater
    b. Column B is greater
    c. The quantities are equal
    d. The relationship cannot be determined

34.

Column A	Column B
65%	5/6

    a. Column A is greater
    b. Column B is greater
    c. The quantities are equal
    d. The relationship cannot be determined

35.

Column A	Column B
.27	25% of .8

    a. Column A is greater
    b. Column B is greater
    c. The quantities are equal
    d. The relationship cannot be determined

Section III - Reading

Questions 1 – 4 refer to the following passage.

Passage 1 When a Poet Longs to Mourn, He Writes an Elegy

Poems are an expressive, especially emotional, form of writing. They have been present in literature virtually from the time civilizations invented the written word. Poets often portrayed as moody, secluded, and even troubled, but this is because poets are introspective and feel deeply about the current events and cultural norms they are surrounded with. Poets often produce the most telling literature, giving insight into the society and mind-set they come from. This can be done in many forms.

The oldest types of poems often include many stanzas, may or may not rhyme, and are more about telling a story than experimenting with language or words. The most common types of ancient poetry are epics, which are usually extremely long stories that follow a hero through his journey, or elegies, which are often solemn in tone and used to mourn or lament something or someone. The Mesopotamians are often said to have invented the written word, and their literature is among the oldest in the world, including the epic poem titled "Epic of Gilgamesh." Similar in style and length to "Gilgamesh" is "Beowulf," an elegy poem written in Old English and set in Scandinavia. These poems are often used by professors as the earliest examples of literature.

The importance of poetry was revived in the Renaissance. At this time, Europeans discovered the style and beauty of ancient Greek arts, and poetry was among those. Shakespeare is the most well-known poet of the time, and he used poetry not only to write poems but also to write plays for the theater. The most popular forms of poetry during the Renaissance included villanelles, sonnets, as well as the epic. Poets during this time focused on style and form, and developed very specific rules and outlines for how an exceptional poem should be written.

As often happens in the arts, modern poets have rejected

the constricting rules of Renaissance poets, and free form poems are much more popular. Some modern poems would read just like stories if they weren't arranged into lines and stanzas. It is difficult to tell which poems and poets will be the most important, because works of art often become more famous in hindsight, after the poet has died and society can look at itself without being in the moment. Modern poetry continues to develop, and will no doubt continue to change as values, thought, and writing continue to change.

Poems can be among the most enlightening and uplifting texts for a person to read if they are looking to connect with the past, connect with other people, or try to gain an understanding of what is happening in their time.

1. In summary, the author has written this passage

    a. as a foreword that will introduce a poem in a book or magazine.

    b. because she loves poetry and wants more people to like it.

    c. to give a brief history of poems.

    d. to convince students to write poems.

2. The author organizes the paragraphs mainly by

    a. moving chronologically, explaining which types of poetry were common in that time.

    b. talking about new types of poems each paragraph and explaining them a little.

    c. focusing on one poet or group of people and the poems they wrote.

    d. explaining older types of poetry so she can talk about modern poetry.

3. The author's claim that poetry has been around "virtually from the time civilizations invented the written word" is supported by the detail that

   a. Beowulf is written in Old English, which is not really in use any longer.

   b. epic poems told stories about heroes.

   c. the Renaissance poets tried to copy Greek poets.

   d. the Mesopotamians are credited with both inventing the word and writing "Epic of Gilgamesh."

4. According to the passage, it can be understood that the word "telling" means

   a. speaking.

   b. significant.

   c. soothing.

   d. wordy.

Questions 5 – 8 refer to the following passage.

Passage 2 - Virus

A virus (from the Latin virus meaning toxin or poison) is a small infectious agent that can replicate only inside the living cells of other organisms. Most viruses are too small to be seen directly with a microscope. Viruses infect all types of organisms, from animals and plants to bacteria and single-celled organisms.

Unlike prions and viroids, viruses consist of two or three parts: all viruses have genes made from either DNA or RNA, all have a protein coat that protects these genes, and some have an envelope of fat that surrounds them when they are outside a cell. (Viroids do not have a protein coat and prions contain no RNA or DNA.) Viruses vary from simple to very complex structures. Most viruses are about one hundred times smaller than an average bacterium. The origins of viruses in the evolutionary history of life are unclear: some may have evolved from plasmids—pieces of DNA that can move between cells—while others may have evolved from bacteria.

Viruses spread in many ways; plant viruses are often transmitted from plant to plant by insects that feed on sap, such as aphids, while animal viruses can be carried by blood-sucking insects. These disease-bearing organisms are known as vectors. Influenza viruses are spread by coughing and sneezing. HIV is one of several viruses transmitted through sexual contact and by exposure to infected blood. Viruses can infect only a limited range of host cells called the "host range." This can be broad as when a virus is capable of infecting many species or narrow. [1]

5. What can we infer from the first paragraph in this selection?

    a. A virus is the same as bacterium.

    b. A person with excellent vision can see a virus with the naked eye.

    c. A virus cannot be seen with the naked eye.

    d. Not all viruses are dangerous.

6. What types of organisms do viruses infect?

    a. Only plants and humans

    b. Only animals and humans

    c. Only disease-prone humans

    d. All types of organisms

7. How many parts do prions and viroids consist of?

    a. Two

    b. Three

    c. Either less than two or more than three

    d. Less than two

8. What is one common virus spread by coughing and sneezing?

    a. AIDS
    b. Influenza
    c. Herpes
    d. Tuberculosis

Questions 9 – 11 refer to the following passage.

Passage 3 – Thunderstorms

The first stage of a thunderstorm is the cumulus stage, or developing stage. In this stage, masses of moisture are lifted upwards into the atmosphere. The trigger for this lift can be insulation heating the ground producing thermals, areas where two winds converge, forcing air upwards, or, where winds blow over terrain of increasing elevation. Moisture in the air rapidly cools into liquid drops of water, which appears as cumulus clouds.

As the water vapor condenses into liquid, latent heat is released which warms the air, causing it to become less dense than the surrounding dry air. The warm air rises in an updraft through the process of convection (hence the term convective precipitation). This creates a low-pressure zone beneath the forming thunderstorm. In a typical thunderstorm, about 5×10^8 kg of water vapor is lifted, and the quantity of energy released when this condenses is about equal to the energy used by a city of 100,000 in a month. [2]

9. The cumulus stage of a thunderstorm is the

    a. The last stage of the storm.
    b. The middle stage of the storm formation.
    c. The beginning of the thunderstorm.
    d. The period after the thunderstorm has ended.

10. One way the air is warmed is

   a. Air moving downwards, which creates a high-pressure zone.

   b. Air cooling and becoming less dense, causing it to rise.

   c. Moisture moving downward toward the earth.

   d. Heat created by water vapor condensing into liquid.

11. Identify the correct sequence of events

   a. Warm air rises, water droplets condense, creating more heat, and the air rises farther.

   b. Warm air rises and cools, water droplets condense, causing low pressure.

   c. Warm air rises and collects water vapor, the water vapor condenses as the air rises, which creates heat, and causes the air to rise farther.

   d. None of the above.

Questions 12 – 14 refer to the following passage.

Passage 4 – US Weather Service

The United States National Weather Service classifies thunderstorms as severe when they reach a predetermined level. Usually, this means the storm is strong enough to inflict wind or hail damage. In most of the United States, a storm is considered severe if winds reach over 50 knots (58 mph or 93 km/h), hail is ¾ inch (2 cm) diameter or larger, or if meteorologists report funnel clouds or tornadoes. In the Central Region of the United States National Weather Service, the hail threshold for a severe thunderstorm is 1 inch (2.5 cm) in diameter. Though a funnel cloud or tornado indicates the presence of a severe thunderstorm, the various meteorological agencies would issue a tornado warning rather than a severe thunderstorm warning here.

Meteorologists in Canada define a severe thunderstorm as

either having tornadoes, wind gusts of 90 km/h or greater, hail 2 centimeters in diameter or greater, rainfall more than 50 millimeters in 1 hour, or 75 millimeters in 3 hours.

Severe thunderstorms can develop from any type of thunderstorm. [3]

12. What is the purpose of this passage?

    a. Explaining when a thunderstorm turns into a tornado.

    b. Explaining who issues storm warnings, and when these warnings should be issued.

    c. Explaining when meteorologists consider a thunderstorm severe.

    d. None of the above.

13. It is possible to infer from this passage that

    a. Different areas and countries have different criteria for determining a severe storm.

    b. Thunderstorms can include lightning and tornadoes, as well as violent winds and large hail.

    c. If someone spots both a thunderstorm and a tornado, meteorological agencies will immediately issue a severe storm warning.

    d. Canada has a much different alert system for severe storms, with criteria that are far less.

14. What would the Central Region of the United States National Weather Service do if hail was 2.7 cm in diameter?

    a. Not issue a severe thunderstorm warning.

    b. Issue a tornado warning.

    c. Issue a severe thunderstorm warning.

    d. Sleet must also accompany the hail before the Weather Service will issue a storm warning.

Questions 15 – 18 refer to the following passage.

Passage 5 – Clouds

A cloud is a visible mass of droplets or frozen crystals floating in the atmosphere above the surface of the Earth or other planetary bodies. Another type of cloud is a mass of material in space, attracted by gravity, called interstellar clouds and nebulae. The branch of meteorology which studies clouds is called nephrology. When we are speaking of Earth clouds, water vapor is usually the condensing substance, which forms small droplets or ice crystal. These crystals are typically 0.01 mm in diameter. Dense, deep clouds reflect most light, so they appear white, at least from the top. Cloud droplets scatter light very efficiently, so the farther into a cloud light travels, the weaker it gets. This accounts for the gray or dark appearance at the base of large clouds. Thin clouds may appear to have acquired the color of their environment or background. [4]

15. What are clouds made of?

a. Water droplets

b. Ice crystals

c. Ice crystals and water droplets

d. Clouds on Earth are made of ice crystals and water droplets

16. The main idea of this passage is

a. Condensation occurs in clouds, having an intense effect on the weather on the surface of the earth.

b. Atmospheric gases are responsible for the gray color of clouds just before a severe storm happens.

c. A cloud is a visible mass of droplets or frozen crystals floating in the atmosphere above the surface of the Earth or other planetary body.

d. Clouds reflect light in varying amounts and degrees, depending on the size and concentration of the water droplets.

17. The branch of meteorology that studies clouds is called

   a. Convection

   b. Thermal meteorology

   c. Nephology

   d. Nephelometry

18. Why are clouds white on top and grey on the bottom?

   a. Because water droplets inside the cloud do not reflect light, it appears white, and the farther into the cloud the light travels, the less light is reflected making the bottom appear dark.

   b. Because water droplets outside the cloud reflect light, it appears dark, and the farther into the cloud the light travels, the more light is reflected making the bottom appear white.

   c. Because water droplets inside the cloud reflects light, making it appear white, and the farther into the cloud the light travels, the more light is reflected making the bottom appear dark.

   d. None of the above.

Questions 19 - 22 refer to the following recipe.

Chocolate Chip Cookies

3/4 cup sugar
3/4 cup packed brown sugar
1 cup butter, softened
2 large eggs, beaten
1 teaspoon vanilla extract
2 1/4 cups all-purpose flour
1 teaspoon baking soda
3/4 teaspoon salt
2 cups semisweet chocolate chips

If desired, 1 cup chopped pecans, or chopped walnuts. Preheat oven to 375 degrees.

Mix sugar, brown sugar, butter, vanilla and eggs in a large bowl. Stir in flour, baking soda, and salt. The dough will be very stiff.

Stir in chocolate chips by hand with a sturdy wooden spoon. Add the pecans, or other nuts, if desired. Stir until the chocolate chips and nuts are evenly dispersed.

Drop dough by rounded tablespoonfuls 2 inches apart onto a cookie sheet.

Bake 8 to 10 minutes or until light brown. Cookies may look underdone, but they will finish cooking after you take them out of the oven.

19. What is the correct order for adding these ingredients?

    a. Brown sugar, baking soda, chocolate chips

    b. Baking soda, brown sugar, chocolate chips

    c. Chocolate chips, baking soda, brown sugar

    d. Baking soda, chocolate chips, brown sugar

20. What does sturdy mean?

    a. Long

    b. Strong

    c. Short

    d. Wide

21. What does disperse mean?

    a. Scatter

    b. To form a ball

    c. To stir

    d. To beat

22. When can you stop stirring the nuts?

   a. When the cookies are cooked
   b. When the nuts are evenly distributed
   c. As soon as the nuts are added
   d. After the chocolate chips are added

Questions 23 – 26 refer to the following passage.

Passage 7 - Ways Characters Communicate in Theater

Playwrights give their characters voices in a way that gives depth and added meaning to what happens on stage during their play. There are different types of speech in scripts that allow characters to talk with themselves, with other characters, and even with the audience.

It is very unique to theater that characters may talk "to themselves." When characters do this, the speech they give is called a soliloquy. Soliloquies are usually poetic, introspective, moving, and can tell audience members about the feelings, motivations, or suspicions of an individual character without that character having to reveal them to other characters on stage. "To be or not to be" is a famous soliloquy given by Hamlet as he considers difficult but important themes, such as life and death.

The most common type of communication in plays is when one character is speaking to another or a group of other characters. This is generally called dialogue, but can also be called monologue if one character speaks without being interrupted for a long time. It is not necessarily the most important type of communication, but it is the most common because the plot of the play cannot really progress without it.

Lastly, and most unique to theater (although it has been used somewhat in film) is when a character speaks directly to the audience. This is called an aside, and scripts usually specifically direct actors to do this. Asides are usually comical, an inside joke between the character and the audience, and very short. The actor will usually face the audience when delivering them, even if it's for a moment, so the audience can recognize this move as an aside.

All three of these types of communication are important to the art of theater, and have been perfected by famous playwrights like Shakespeare. Understanding these types of communication can help an audience member grasp what is artful about the script and action of a play.

23. According to the passage, characters in plays communicate to

    a. move the plot forward.

    b. show the private thoughts and feelings of one character.

    c. make the audience laugh.

    d. add beauty and artistry to the play.

24. When Hamlet delivers "To be or not to be," he can most likely be described as

    a. solitary.

    b. thoughtful.

    c. dramatic.

    d. hopeless.

25. The author uses parentheses to punctuate "although it has been used somewhat in film,"

    a. to show that films are less important.

    b. instead of using commas so that the sentence is not interrupted.

    c. because parenthesis help separate details that are not as important.

    d. to show that films are not as artistic.

26. It can be understood that by the phrase "give their characters voices," the author means that

   a. playwrights are generous.

   b. playwrights are changing the sound or meaning of characters' voices to fit what they had in mind.

   c. dialogue is important in creating characters.

   d. playwrights may be the parent of one of their actors and literally give them their voice.

Questions 27 – 30 refer to the following passage.

Passage 8 – Navy SEAL

The United States Navy's Sea, Air and Land Teams, commonly known as Navy SEALs, are the U.S. Navy's principle special operations force, and a part of the Naval Special Warfare Command (NSWC) as well as the maritime component of the United States Special Operations Command (USSOCOM).

The unit's acronym ("SEAL") comes from their capacity to operate at sea, in the air, and on land – but it is their ability to work underwater that separates SEALs from most other military units in the world. Navy SEALs are trained and have been deployed in a wide variety of missions, including direct action and special reconnaissance operations, unconventional warfare, foreign internal defence, hostage rescue, counter-terrorism and other missions. All SEALs are members of either the United States Navy or the United States Coast Guard.

In the early morning of May 2, 2011 local time, a team of 40 CIA-led Navy SEALs completed an operation to kill Osama bin Laden in Abbottabad, Pakistan about 35 miles (56 km) from Islamabad, the country's capital. The Navy SEALs were part of the Naval Special Warfare Development Group, previously called "Team 6." President Barack Obama later confirmed the death of bin Laden. The unprecedented media coverage raised the public profile of the SEAL community, particularly the counter-terrorism specialists commonly known as SEAL Team 6. [5]

27. Are Navy SEALs part of USSOCOM?

a. Yes

b. No

c. Only for special operations

d. No, they are part of the US Navy

28. What separates Navy SEALs from other military units?

a. Belonging to NSWC

b. Direct action and special reconnaissance operations

c. Working underwater

d. Working for other military units in the world

29. What other military organizations do SEALs belong to?

a. The US Navy

b. The Coast Guard

c. The US Army

d. The Navy and the Coast Guard

30. What other organization participated in the Bin Laden raid?

a. The CIA

b. The US Military

c. Counter-terrorism specialists

d. None of the above

Questions 31 – 34 refer to the following passage.

Passage 9 - Gardening

Gardening for food extends far into prehistory. Ornamental gardens were known in ancient times, a famous example being the Hanging Gardens of Babylon, while ancient Rome had dozens of gardens.
The earliest forms of gardens emerged from the people's need to grow herbs and vegetables. It was only later that rich individuals created gardens for purely decorative purposes.

In ancient Egypt, rich people created ornamental gardens to relax in the shade of the trees. Egyptians believed that gods liked gardens. Commonly, walls surrounded ancient Egyptian gardens with trees planted in rows.

The most popular tree species were date palms, sycamores, fig trees, nut trees, and willows. Besides ornamental gardens, wealthy Egyptians kept vineyards to produce wine.

The Assyrians are also known for their beautiful gardens in what we know today as Iraq. Assyrian gardens were very large, with some of them used for hunting and others as leisure gardens. Cypress and palm were the most popular trees in Assyrian gardens. [6]

31. Why did wealthy people in Egypt have gardens?

   a. For food
   b. To relax in the shade
   c. For ornamentation
   d. For hunting

32. What did the Egyptians believe about gardens?

    a. They believed gods loved gardens.

    b. They believed gods hated gardens.

    c. The didn't have any beliefs about gods and Gardens.

    d. They believed gods hated trees.

33. What kinds of trees did the Assyrians like?

    a. The Assyrians liked date palms, sycamores, fig trees, nut trees, and willows.

    b. The Assyrians liked Cypresses and palms.

    c. The Assyrians didn't like trees.

    d. The Assyrians liked hedges and vines.

34. Which came first, gardening for vegetables or ornamental gardens?

    a. Ornamental gardens came before vegetable gardens.

    b. Vegetable gardens came before ornamental gardens.

    c. Vegetable and ornamental gardens appeared at the same time.

    d. The passage does not give enough information.

Questions 35 – 36 refer to the following passage.

Passage 10 - Gardens

Ancient Roman gardens are known for their statues and sculptures, which were never missing from the lives of Romans. Romans designed their gardens with hedges and vines as well as a wide variety of flowers, including acanthus, cornflowers and crocus, cyclamen, hyacinth, iris and ivy, lavender, lilies, myrtle, narcissus, poppy, rosemary and violet. Flower beds were popular in the courtyards of the rich Romans.

The Middle Ages was a period of decline in gardening. After the fall of Rome, gardening was only to growing medicinal herbs and decorating church altars.

Islamic gardens were built after the model of Persian gardens, with enclosed walls and watercourses dividing the garden into four. Commonly, the center of the garden would have a pool or pavilion. Mosaics and glazed tiles used to decorate elaborate fountains are specific to Islamic gardens.
6

35. What is a characteristic feature of Roman gardens?

    a. Statues and sculptures

    b. Flower beds

    c. Medicinal herbs

    d. Courtyard gardens

36. When did gardening decline?

    a. Before the Fall of Rome

    b. Gardening did not decline

    c. Before the Middle Ages

    d. After the Fall of Rome

Questions 37 – 40 refer to the following passage.

Passage 11 - Winged Victory of Samothrace: the Statue of the Gods

Students who read about the "Winged Victory of Samothrace" probably won't be able to picture what this statue looks like. However, almost anyone who knows a little about statues will recognize it when they see it: it is the statue of a winged woman who does not have arms or a head. Even the most famous pieces of art may be recognized by sight but not by name.

This iconic statue is of the Greek goddess Nike, who represented victory and was called Victoria by the Romans.

The statue is sometimes called the "Nike of Samothrace." She was often displayed in Greek art as driving a chariot, and her speed or efficiency with the chariot may be what her wings symbolize. It is said that the statue was created around 200 BCE to celebrate a battle that was won at sea. Archaeologists and art historians believe the statue may have originally been part of a temple or other building, even one of the most important temples, Megaloi Theoi, just as many statues were used during that time.

"Winged Victory" does indeed appear to have had arms and a head when it was originally created, and it is unclear why they were removed or lost. Indeed, they have never been discovered, even with all the excavation that has taken place. Many speculate that one of her arms was raised and put to her mouth, as though she was shouting or calling out, which is consistent with the idea of her as a war figure. If the missing pieces were ever to be found, they might give Greek and art historians more of an idea of what Nike represented or how the statue was used.

Learning about pieces of art through details like these can help students remember time frames or locations, as well as learn about the people who occupied them.

37. The author's title says the statue is "of the Gods" because

    a. the statue is very beautiful and even a god would find it beautiful.

    b. the statue is of a Greek goddess, and gods were of primary importance to the Greek.

    c. Nike lead the gods into war.

    d. the statues were used at the temple of the gods and so it belonged to them.

38. The third paragraph states that

   a. the statue is related to war and was probably broken apart by foreign soldiers.

   b. the arms and head of the statue cannot be found because all the excavation has taken place.

   c. speculations have been made about what the entire statue looked like and what it symbolized.

   d. the statue has no arms or head because the sculptor lost them.

39. The author's main purpose in writing this passage is to

   a. demonstrate that art and culture are related and one can teach us about the other

   b. persuade readers to become archeologists and find the missing pieces of the statue

   c. teach readers about the Greek goddess Nike

   d. to teach readers the name of a statue they probably recognize

40. The author specifies the indirect audience as "students" because

   a. it is probably a student who is taking this test

   b. most young people don't know much about art yet and most young people are students

   c. students read more than people who are not students

   d. the passage is based on a discussion of what we can learn about culture from art

Section IV – Math

1. Simplify 2 1/3 / 1 2/5

    a. 1 2/5
    b. 1 2/3
    c. 1 1/7
    d. 2 2/5

2. 2/3 x 1 4/7 x 5 1/4

    a. 3 1/4
    b. 5 1/2
    c. 6 2/3
    d. 4 2/5

3. Simplify 4 1/5 / 2 1/3

    a. 1 4/5
    b. 2 1/4
    c. 1 3/7
    d. 2 1/4

4. 10/3 x 2 1/4 x 3 1/5

    a. 1 3/4
    b. 24
    c. 7 2/7
    d. 5 1/5

5. Simplify 3 1/9 / 2 2/3

    a. 2 1/5
    b. 2 3/4
    c. 1 1/6
    d. 1 1/4

6. What is -9 + (+6) − (-2)

    a. -3
    b. -1
    c. 5
    d. -5

7. Smith and Simon are playing a card game. Smith will win if a card drawn from a deck of 52 is either a 7 or a diamond, and Simon will win if the drawn card is an even number. Which statement is more likely to be correct?

    a. Simon will win more games.
    b. Smith will win more games.
    c. They have same winning probability.
    d. A decision cannot be made from the provided data.

8. By practicing, a typist increases his typing speed by 2 words per minute daily. If his current typing speed is 18 words per minute and he practice 3 hours a day, then how many hours will he need to practice to attain 40 words per minute?

    a. 27
    b. 30
    c. 33
    d. 36

9. If the speed of a train is 72 kilometers per hour, what distance will it cover in 12 seconds?

    a. 200 m
    b. 220 m
    c. 240 m
    d. 260 m

10. In a class of 83 students, 72 are present. What percent of the students are absent? Provide answer up to two significant digits.

   a. 12
   b. 13
   c. 14
   d. 15

11. A driver traveled from city A to city B in 1 hour and 13 minutes. On the way, he had to stop at 5 traffic signals, with an average time of 80 seconds. If the distance between the cities is 65 kilometers then what was the average driving speed?

   a. 56.42
   b. 58.77
   c. 60.34
   d. 63.25

12. Mr. Micheal runs a factory. His total assets are $256,800 that consists of a building worth $80,500, machinery worth $125.000 and $51,300 cash. After one year what will be the value of his total assets if he has additional cash of $75,600 and the value of his building has increased by 10% per year, and his machinery depreciated by 20% per year?

   a. $24,3450
   b. $25,2450
   c. $26,4150
   d. $27,2350

13. Martin earns $25,000 as basic pay, $500 rent and $860 for medical insurance. He spends 40% of his total earning on food and clothing, 10% on children's education and pays $800 for utility bills. What percent of his earning he is saving?

   a. 54%
   b. 50%
   c. 47%
   d. 44%

14. Prize money of $1,050 is to be shared among top three contestants in ratio of 7:5:3 as 1st, 2nd and 3rd prizes respectively. How much more money will the 1st prize contestant receive than the 3rd prize contestant?

   a. $210
   b. $280
   c. $350
   d. $490

15. The manager of a weaving factory estimates that if 10 machines run on 100% efficiency for 8 hours, they will produce 1450 meters of cloth. Due to some technical problems, 4 machines run of 95% efficiency and the remaining 6 at 90% efficiency. How many meters of cloth can these machines will produce in 8 hours?

   a. 1334 meters
   b. 1310 meters
   c. 1300 meters
   d. 1285 meters

16. A car covers a distance in 3.5 hours at an average speed of 60 km/hr. How much time in hours will a motorbike take to cover this distance at an average speed of 40km/hr?

    a. 4.5
    b. 4.75
    c. 5
    d. 5.25

17. A grandfather is 8 times older than his grandson is now. After 6 years, he will be 5 times older than his grandson will. How old is the grandfather now?

    a. 48
    b. 56
    c. 64
    d. 72

18. Solve for n. $5n + (19 - 2)) = 67$.

    a. 21
    b. 10
    c. 15
    d. 7

19. A boy is given 2 apples while his sister is given 8 oranges. What is the ratio between his apples and her oranges?

    a. 1:2
    b. 2:4
    c. 1:4
    d. 2:1

20. A box contains 7 black pencils and 28 blue ones. What is the ratio between the black and blue pens?

    a. 1:4
    b. 2:7
    c. 1:8
    d. 1:9

21. If X + (32 + 356) = 920. What is x?

    a. 450
    b. 388
    c. 532
    d. 623

22. A boy buys 10 candies. The packet contains 3 green candies, 12 red and 9 blue candies. What is the ratio the green, red and blue sweets?

    a. 1:3:4
    b. 1:4:3
    c. 2:3:1
    d. 1:5:4

23. Solve for x. (12 x 12)/x = 12

    a. 12
    b. 13
    c. 8
    d. 14

24. Solve for A. A − (34 x 2) = 18.

    a. 86
    b. 78
    c. 50
    d. 73

25. Solve for X.   X% of 120 = 30.

    a. 15
    b. 12
    c. 4
    d. 25

26. Solve for X. X * 25% of 100 = 76.

    a. 15
    b. 19
    c. 21
    d. 13

27. Solve for X. X% of 250 = 50.

    a. 30
    b. 35
    c. 25
    d. 20

28. What is the least common multiple of 4 and 3?

    a. 24
    b. 6
    c. 16
    d. 12

29. What is the ratio between 2 gold coins, 6 silver coins and 12 bronze coins?

    a. 2:3:4
    b. 1:2:4
    c. 1:3:4
    d. 2:3:4

30. What is the least common multiple of 8 and 12?

    a. 24
    b. 36
    c. 12
    d. 8

31. Solve for x. -7 + 3x = 20.

    a. 7
    b. 5
    c. 4
    d. 9

32. What is the least common multiple of 2 and 3?

    a. 2
    b. 4
    c. 6
    d. 3

33. Solve for c, when 124 = 12c - 20.

    a. 6
    b. 12
    c. 10
    d. 15

34. Simplify 3 8/9 + 5 5/6.

    a. 8 13/15
    b. 8 3/9
    c. 9 13/18
    d. 8 12/18

35. Simplify 7 4/5 + 2 2/5.

    a. 5 3/5
    b. 5 1/5
    c. 4 2/5
    d. 5 2/5

36. Translate the following into an equation: three plus a number times 7 equals 42.

    a. $7(3 + X) = 42$
    b. $3(X + 7) = 42$
    c. $3X + 7 = 42$
    d. $(3 + 7)X = 42$

37. Estimate 5205 / 25

    a. 108
    b. 308
    c. 208
    d. 408

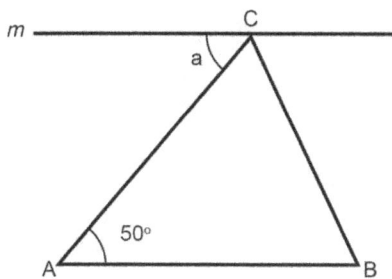

38. If the line m is parallel to the side AB of △ABC, what is angle a?

    a. 130°
    b. 25°
    c. 65°
    d. 50°

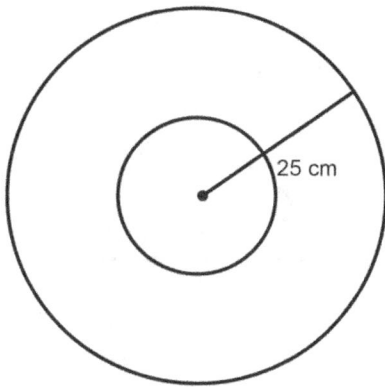

Note: Figure not drawn to scale

39. What is the distance travelled by the wheel above, when it makes 175 revolutions?

    a. 87.5 π m
    b. 875 π m
    c. 8.75 π m
    d. 8750 π m

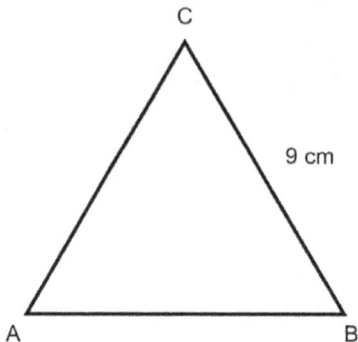

Note: Figure not drawn to scale

40. What is the perimeter of the equilateral △ABC above?

    a. 18 cm
    b. 12 cm
    c. 27 cm
    d. 15 cm

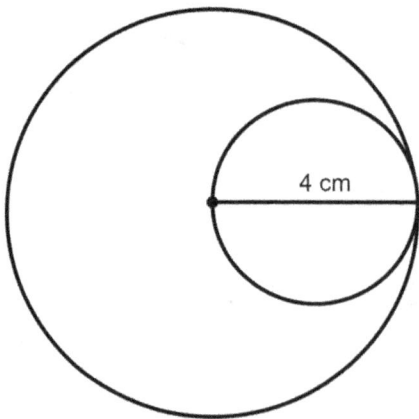

Note: figure not drawn to scale

41. Assuming the diameter of the small circle is the radius of the large circle, what is (area of large circle) - (area of small circle) in the figure above?

    a. 8 π cm²
    b. 10 π cm²
    c. 12 π cm²
    d. 16 π cm²

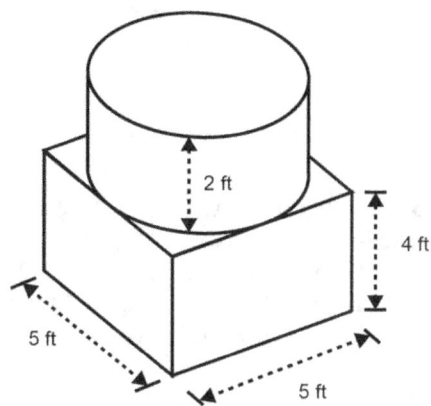

Note: figure not drawn to scale

42. What is the approximate total volume of the above solid?

    a. 120 ft³
    b. 100 ft³
    c. 140 ft³
    d. 160 ft³

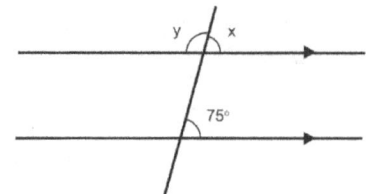

43. What is the value of the angle y?

   a. 25°
   b. 15°
   c. 30°
   d. 105°

44. In a local election at polling station A, 945 voters cast their vote out of 1270 registered voters. At polling station B, 860 cast their vote out of 1050 registered voters and at station C, 1210 cast their vote out of 1440 registered voters. What is the total turnout including all three polling stations?

   a. 70%
   b. 74%
   c. 76%
   d. 80%

45. 3a + 4b x d =? When A = 2, b = 4 and d = 8.

   a. 40
   b. 90
   c. 80
   d. 65

Answer Key

Section I - Verbal Reasoning

1. B
Peculiar and strange are synonyms.

2. B
Tippet and shawl are synonyms.

3. D
Vivid and brilliant are synonyms.

4. B
Semblance and image are synonyms.

5. A
Impregnable and unconquerable are synonyms.

6. A
Jargon and slang are synonyms.

7. A
Render and give are synonyms.

8. B
Intrusive and invasive are synonyms.

9. A
Renowned and popular are synonyms.

10. C
Incoherent and jumbled are synonyms.

11. A
Congenial and pleasant are synonyms.

12. D
Plight and situation are synonyms.

13. A
Berate and criticize are synonyms.

14. C
Construe and interpret are synonyms.

15. D
Scared and terrified are synonyms.

16. A
Demonstrated and presented are synonyms.

17. C
Halt and stop are synonyms.

18. C
Strange and unfamiliar are synonyms.

19. D
Seize and win are synonyms.

20. B
Divulge and tell are synonyms.

21. C
Convection NOUN the vertical movement of heat and moisture.

22. B
Ethanol NOUN a type of alcohol used as fuel.

23. A
Respiratory NOUN relating to respiration; breathing.

24. C
Renewable NOUN capable of being renewed.

25. B
Combustible NOUN capable of burning.

26. D
Conclusive ADJECTIVE providing an end to something; decisive.

27. D
Deftly ADVERB quickly and neatly in action.

28. C
Dupe VERB to swindle, deceive, or trick.

29. D
Designate ADJECTIVE appointed; chosen.

30. A
Dispel VERB to drive away by scattering, or so to cause to vanish; to clear away.

31. B
Frugal ADJECTIVE cheap, economical, thrifty.

22. B
Baubles NOUN a cheap showy ornament.

33. D
Creditors NOUN a person to whom a debt is owed.

34. A
Oratory NOUN the art of public speaking, especially in a formal, expressive, or forceful manner.

35. B
Liquidate VERB to convert assets into cash.

36. A
Hoax NOUN to deceive (someone) by making them believe something which has been maliciously or mischievously fabricated.

37. C
Defective ADJECTIVE imperfect or faulty.

38. B
Grovel VERB to abase oneself before another person.

39. B
Intolerable ADJECTIVE not capable of being borne or endured; not proper or right to be allowed; insufferable; insupportable; unbearable.

40. A
Heirloom NOUN A valued possession that has been passed down through the generations.

Section II – Quantitative Reasoning

1. B
5x + 21 = 66, 5x = 66 – 21 = 45, 5x = 45, x = 45/5 = 9

2. B
Multiples of 3 are 3, 6, 9 and Multiples of 9 are 9, 18, therefore the least common multiple is 9.

3. A
The formula for the volume of a cylinder is = $\prod$; r²h. Where $\prod$ is 3.142, r is radius of the cross sectional area, and h is the height. So the volume will be = 3.142 × 2.52 × 12 = 235.65 m³.

4. B
215 X 65 = 13,975, or approximately 13,500.

5. D
We understand that each of the n employees earn s amount of salary weekly. This means that one employee earns s salary weekly. So; Richard has ns amount of money to employ n employees for a week.

We are asked to find the number of days n employees can be employed with x amount of money. We can do simple direct proportion:

If Richard can employ n employees for 7 days with ns amount of money,

Richard can employ n employees for y days with x amount of money ... y is the number of days we need to find.

We can do cross multiplication:

y = (x•7)/(ns)

y = 7x/ns

6. B
Average attendance will be 85%

7. B
A driver at a speed of 's' miles per hour can reach his destination in 'h' hours. If his speed increased from 's' to 'x', the driver will reach the destination in h - sh/x hours.

8. B
The number is 41.061. The last digit 1 is less than 5, and so it's discarded. The next digit, 6, is greater than 5 and so is removed and 1 is added to the next digit to the left. Answer = 41.1

9. C
If there are 5 friends and each drink costs $1.89, we can round up to $2 per drink and estimate the total cost at, 5 X $2 = $10.

The actual cost is 5 X $1.89 = $9.45.

10. C
Ratio of people sitting to standing is 24:8, reduce to lowest terms = 3:1

11. A
4,210,987 – 210,078 = 4,000,909, or about 4,000,000.

12. A
$2^3 = 8 = 1/0.125$

$\sqrt{16} = 4$
$3^2 = 9$

13. B
10^4 is not equal to $0.1 \times 10^5 = 10,000$.

14. D
Divide x^5 by $x^2 = x^3$

15. D
21/28 is the only fraction not equivalent to 3/4.

16. C
3/2 = 1.5
√2 = 1.414213
4/3 = 1.333

17. A
1/4 X 100 = 25
25 X 5 = 125

18. C
3X + 3 = 15
X = 4
A – 20 – 4 = 16
B – 4 * $ = 16

19. B
2Y + X will be greater than 2X + Y for any X>0 and Y>0.

20. C
$y^2 + 6 = 15$
Y = 3

21. D
2ab + 5 = 25
ab = 10
a could be greater or less than 14 (e.g. a = 50 and b = 1/5) or less than 14 (e.g. a = 2 and b = 5).

22. B
0.589/.35 = 1.6828 > 1/2

23. B
.589/.35 = 1.6828 > 2/3.

24. A
4/9 + 3/4 = 43/36 > 24/27

25. B
250 – 20% = 200 – 2% = 196
Total Savings is 250 – 196 = 54.

26. A
X = 135/50 = 2.7 hours < 3.1 hours.

27. B
1 hr. = 60 minutes, at the rate of 1 page per 2 minutes, 60/2 = 30 < 40.

28. B
2X $3 + 1.99 + 1.58 = 9.57 + 3.2% = 9.876 or $9.88
20 − 9.88 = $10.12

29. B
Building: $580,000 + 5.6% = 612,480
Machinery: $255,000 − 15% = 216,750
Cash: $10,000 + 4500 = 14500
Total after 1 year = 643,730

30. A
4% interest is earned in the first year on the initial deposit of $500. In the second year, interest is earned on the initial deposit and the interest earned in the first year.
500 + 4% = 520
520 + 4% = 540.80

$20 was earned in the first year and $20.80 in the second year for a total of $40.80

31. B
(5 + 8 + 2 + 0 + 4)/5 = 3.8

32. B
3/4 = 75% < 80%

33. B
.78 as a fraction = 78/100 < 8/10

34. B
5/6 = 83/100 (approx.) = 83% > 65%

35. A
25% of .8 = .2 < .27

Section III – Reading

1. C
This question tests the reader's summarizing skills. The use of the word "actually" in describing what kind of people poets are, as well as other moments like this, may lead readers to selecting B or D, but the author is giving more information than trying to persuade readers. The author gives no indication that she loves poetry (B) or that people, students specifically (D), should write poems. A is incorrect because the style and content of this paragraph do not match those of a foreword; forewords usually focus on the history or ideas of a specific poem to introduce it more fully and help it stand out against other poems. The author here focuses on several poems and gives broad statements. Instead, she tells a kind of story about poems, giving three very broad time periods in which to discuss them, thereby giving a brief history of poetry, as answer C states.

2. A
This question tests the reader's summarizing skills. Key words in the topic sentences of each of the paragraphs ("oldest," "Renaissance," "modern") should give the reader an idea that the author is moving chronologically. The opening and closing sentence-paragraphs are broad and talk generally. B seems reasonable, but epic poems are mentioned in two paragraphs, eliminating the idea that only new types of poems are used in each paragraph. C is also easily eliminated because the author clearly mentions several different poets, groups of people, and poems. D also seems reasonable, considering that the author does move from older forms of poetry to newer forms, but use of "so (that)" makes this statement false, for the author gives no indication that she is rushing (the paragraphs are about the same size) or that she prefers modern poetry.

3. D
This question tests the reader's attention to detail. The key word is "invented"--it ties together the Mesopotamians, who invented the written word, and the fact that they, as the inventors, also invented and used poetry. The other selections focus on other details mentioned in the passage, such as

that the Renaissance's admiration of the Greeks (C) and that Beowulf is in Old English (A). B may seem like an attractive answer because it is unlike the others and because the idea of heroes seems rooted in ancient and early civilizations.

4. B
This question tests the reader's vocabulary and contextualization skills. "Telling" is not an unusual word, but it may be used here in a way that is not familiar to readers, as an adjective rather than a verb in gerund form. A may seem like the obvious answer to a reader looking for a verb to match the use they are familiar with. If the reader understands that the word is being used as an adjective and that A is a ploy, they may opt to select D, "wordy," but it does not make sense in context. C can be easily eliminated, and doesn't have any connection to the paragraph or passage. "Significant" (B) does make sense contextually, especially in relation to the phrase "give insight" used later in the sentence.

5. C
We can infer from the passage that, a virus is too small to be seen with the naked eye. Clearly, if they are too small to be seen with a microscope, then they are too small to be seen with the naked eye.

6. D
Viruses infect all types of organisms. This is taken directly from the passage, "Viruses infect all types of organisms, from animals and plants to bacteria and single-celled organisms."

7. C
The passage does not say exactly how many parts prions and viroids consist of. It does say, "**Unlike** prions and viroids, viruses consist of two or three parts ..." so prions and viroids are NOT like virus. We can therefore infer, they consist of either less than two or more than three parts.

8. B
A common virus spread by coughing and sneezing is Influenza.

9. C
The cumulus stage of a thunderstorm is the beginning of the

thunderstorm.

This is taken directly from the passage, "The first stage of a thunderstorm is the cumulus, or developing stage."

10. D
The passage lists four ways that air is heated. One way is, heat created by water vapor condensing into liquid.

11. A
The sequence of events can be taken from these sentences:

As the moisture carried by the [1] air currents rises, it rapidly cools into liquid drops of water, which appear as cumulus clouds. As the water vapor condenses into liquid, it [2] releases heat, which warms the air. This in turn causes the air to become less dense than the surrounding dry air and [3] rise farther.

12. C
The purpose of this text is to explain when meteorologists consider a thunderstorm severe.

The main idea is the first sentence, "The United States National Weather Service classifies thunderstorms as severe when they reach a predetermined level." After the first sentence, the passage explains and elaborates on this idea. Everything is this passage is related to this idea, and there are no other major ideas in this passage that are central to the whole passage.

13. A
From this passage, we can infer that different areas and countries have different criteria for determining a severe storm.

From the passage we can see that most of the US has a criteria of, winds over 50 knots (58 mph or 93 km/h), and hail ¾ inch (2 cm). For the Central US, hail must be 1 inch (2.5 cm) in diameter. In Canada, winds must be 90 km/h or greater, hail 2 centimeters in diameter or greater, and rainfall more than 50 millimeters in 1 hour, or 75 millimeters in 3 hours.

Choice D is incorrect because the Canadian system is the same for hail, 2 centimeters in diameter.

14. C
With hail above the minimum size of 2.5 cm. diameter, the Central Region of the United States National Weather Service would issue a severe thunderstorm warning.

15. D
Clouds in space are made of different materials attracted by gravity. Clouds on Earth are made of water droplets or ice crystals.

Choice D is the best answer. Notice also that Choice D is the most specific.

16. C
The main idea is the first sentence of the passage; a cloud is a visible mass of droplets or frozen crystals floating in the atmosphere above the surface of the Earth or other planetary body.

The main idea is very often the first sentence of the paragraph.

17. C
Nephology, which is the study of cloud physics.

18. C
This question asks about the process, and gives choices that can be confirmed or eliminated easily.

From the passage, "Dense, deep clouds reflect most light, so they appear white, at least from the top. Cloud droplets scatter light very efficiently, so the farther into a cloud light travels, the weaker it gets. This accounts for the gray or dark appearance at the base of large clouds."

We can eliminate choice A, since water droplets inside the cloud do not reflect light is false.

We can eliminate choice B, since, water droplets outside the cloud reflect light, it appears dark, is false.

Choice C is correct.

19. A
The correct order of ingredients is brown sugar, baking soda and chocolate chips.

20. B
Sturdy: strong, solid in structure or person. In context, Stir in chocolate chips by hand with a *sturdy* wooden spoon.

21. A
Disperse: to scatter in different directions or break up. In context, Stir until the chocolate chips and nuts are evenly *dispersed*.

22. B
You can stop stirring the nuts when they are evenly distributed. From the passage, "Stir until the chocolate chips and nuts are evenly dispersed."

23. D
This question tests the reader's summarization skills. The question is asking very generally about the message of the passage, and the title, "Ways Characters Communicate in Theater," is one indication of that. The other answers A, B, and C are all directly from the text, and therefore readers may be inclined to select one of them, but are too specific to encapsulate the entirety of the passage and its message.

24. B
The paragraph on soliloquies mentions "To be or not to be," and it is from the context of that paragraph that readers may understand that because "To be or not to be" is a soliloquy, Hamlet will be introspective, or thoughtful, while delivering it. It is true that actors deliver soliloquies alone, and may be "solitary" (A), but "thoughtful" (B) is more true to the overall idea of the paragraph. Readers may choose C because drama and theater can be used interchangeably and the passage mentions that soliloquies are unique to theater (and therefore drama), but this answer is not specific enough to the paragraph in question. Readers may pick up on the theme of life and death and Hamlet's true intentions and select that he is "hopeless" (D), but those themes are not discussed either by this paragraph or passage, as a close textual reading and analysis confirms.

25. C
This question tests the reader's grammatical skills. B seems logical, but parenthesis are actually considered to be a stronger break in a sentence than commas are, and along this line of thinking, actually disrupt the sentence more. A and D make comparisons between theater and film that are simply not made in the passage, and may or may not be true. This detail does clarify the statement that asides are most unique to theater by adding that it is not completely unique to theater, which may have been why the author didn't chose not to delete it and instead used parentheses to designate the detail's importance (C).

26. C
This question tests the reader's vocabulary and contextualization skills. A may or may not be true, but focuses on the wrong function of the word "give" and ignores the rest of the sentence, which is more relevant to what the passage is discussing. B and D may also be selected if the reader depends too literally on the word "give," failing to grasp the more abstract function of the word that is the focus of answer C, which also properly acknowledges the entirety of the passage and its meaning.

27. A
Navy SEALS are the maritime component of the United States Special Operations Command (USSOCOM).

28. C
Working underwater separates SEALs from other military units. This is taken directly from the passage.

29. D
SEALs also belong to the Navy and the Coast Guard.

30. A
The CIA also participated. From the passage, the raid was conducted by a "team of 40 *CIA-led* Navy SEALS."

31. B
This question is taken directly from the passage. Scan the passage for the word "Egypt" to find the answer quickly.

32. A
The Egyptians believed gods loved gardens.

33. B
Cypresses and palms were the most popular trees in Assyrian Gardens.

34. B
Vegetable gardens came before ornamental gardens.

The earliest forms of gardens emerged from the people's need to grow herbs and vegetables. It was only later that rich individuals created gardens for the purely decorative purpose.

35. A
The ancient Roman gardens are known by their statues and sculptures ... from the first sentence.

36. D
After the fall of Rome, gardening was only for medicinal purposes, AND gardening declined in the Middle Ages, so we can infer gardening declined after the fall of Rome.

37. B
This question tests the reader's summarization skills. A is a very broad statement that may or may not be true, and seems to be in context, but has nothing to do with the passage. The author does mention that the statue was probably used on a temple dedicated to the Greek gods (D), but in no way discusses or argues for the gods' attitude toward or claim on these temples or its faucets. Nike does indeed lead the gods into a war (the Titan war), as C suggests, but this is not mentioned by the passage and students who know this may be drawn to this answer but have not done a close enough analysis of the text that is actually in the passage. B is appropriately expository, and connects the titular emphasis to the idea that the Greek gods are very important to Greek culture.

38. C
This question tests the reader's summarization skills. The test for question C is pulled straight from the paragraph, but is not word for word, so it may seem too obvious to be the right answer. The passage does talk about Nike being the goddess of war, as A states, but the third paragraph only touches on it and it is an inference that soldiers destroyed

the statue, when this question is asking specifically for what the third paragraph actually stated. B is also straight from the text, with a minor but key change: the inclusion of the words "all" and "never" are too limiting and the passage does not suggest that these limits exist. If a reader selects D, they are also making an inference that is misguided for this type of question. The paragraph does state that the arms and head are "lost" but does not suggest who lost them.

39. A
This question tests the reader's ability to recognize function in writing. B can be eliminated based on the purpose of the passage, which is expository and not persuasive. The author may or may not feel this way, but the passage does not show evidence of being argumentative for that purpose. C and D are both details found in the text, but neither of them encompasses the entire message of the passage, which has an overall message of learning about culture from art and making guesses about how the two are related, as suggested by A.

40. D
This question tests the reader's ability to understand function within writing. Most of the possible selections are very general statements which may or may not be true. It probably is a student who is taking the test on which this question is featured (A), but the author makes no address to the test taker and is not talking to the audience in terms of the test. Likewise, it may also be true that students read more than adults (C), mandated by schools and grades, but the focus on the verb "read" in the first sentence is too narrow and misses the larger purpose of the passage; the same could be said for selection B. While all the statements could be true, D is the most germane, and infers the purpose of the passage without making assumptions that could be incorrect.

Section IV – Mathematics

1. B
First change all the terms to fractions, therefore, we get $7/3 / 7/5$, to divide we need to invert the second fraction, $7/3 \times 5/7$, and then we cancel out to reduce to the lowest terms,

1/3 x 5/1 = 5/3, convert back to proper fraction to get 1 2/3

2. B
First, convert all the terms to fractions and then cancel out.
Therefore, 2/3 x 11/7 x 21/4 = 2/3 x 11/1 x 3/4, 1/3 x 11/1 x 3/2, 1/1 x 11/1 x 1/2 = 11/2 = 5 1/2

3. A
First change all the terms to fractions, therefore, we get 21/5 / 7/3, to divide we need to invert the second fraction, 21/5 x 3/7, and then we cancel out to reduce to the lowest terms, 3/5 x 3/1 = 9/5, convert back to proper fraction to get 1 4/5

4. B
First, convert all the terms to fractions and then cancel out.
Therefore, 10/3 x 9/4 x 16/5 = 10/1 x 3/4 x 16/5, 10/1 x 3/1 x 4/5, 2/1 x 3/1 x 4/1 = 24/1 = 24

5. C
First change all the terms to fractions, 28/9 / 8/3, to divide we need to invert the second fraction, 28/9 x 3/8, and then we cancel out to reduce to the lowest terms, 7/3 x 1/2 = 7/6, convert back to proper fraction to get 1 1/6

6. B
+(+) becomes a positive sign and -(-) equals +, therefore -9 + (+6) – (-2) = -9 + 6 + 2 = -3 + 2 = -1

7. B
There are 52 cards. Smith has 16 cards in which he can win. Therefore, his winning probability in a single game will be 16/52. Simon has 20 cards of wining so his probability of winning in single draw is 20/52. Simon will win more games.

8. C
This is an arithmetic series question where the 1st term is 18 and last term is 40. Expressing the question as a series, we have

18, 20, 22, 24, 26, 28, 30, 32, 34, 36, 38, 40
Therefore, after 11 days of practice he attains that 40 word per minute. As he practices 3 hours daily, the total number

of hours required will be 33.

9. C
1 hour is equal to 3600 seconds and 1 kilometer is equal to 1000 meters. Therefore, a train covers 72000 meters in 36000 seconds.
Distance covered in 12 seconds = 12 × 72000/3600 = 240 meters.

10. B
Number of absent students = 83 − 72 = 11

Percentage of absent students is found by proportioning the number of absent students to total number of students in the class = 11•100/83 = 13.25

Checking the answers, we round 13.25 to the nearest whole number: 13%

Day	Absent	Present	% Attendance
Monday	5	40	88.88%
Tuesday	9	36	80.00%
Wednesday	4	41	91.11%
Thursday	10	35	77.77%
Friday	6	39	86.66%

11. B
Time taken to travel from A to B in seconds = 3600 + (13 X 60) = 3600 + 780 = 4380 seconds.
Total time spent at traffic signals = 80 X 5 = 400 seconds.
The remaining driving time = 4380 − 400 = 3980 seconds = 3980/3600 = 1.106 hours
The speed will be 65/1.106 = 58.77 km/hr

12. C
Cash assets = 75600
Building assets after one year = 80500 X 1.1 = $88550
Machinery assets after one year = 125000 X 0.8 = 100,000
Total value of assets = 264150

13. C
Total earnings = 25000 + 500 + 860 = $26360
Food and Clothing expenses = 0.4 X 26360 = 10544

Children's education expense = 26360 X 0.1 = $2636
Utility Bills = $800
Savings = 26360 – 10544 – 2636 – 800 = $12380
Percent savings = 100 X 12380/26360 = 47%

14. B
1st prize winner receives, 7 X 1050/15 = $490
3rd price winner receives, 3 X 1050/15 = $210
Difference = 490 – 210 = $280

15. A
At 100% efficiency 1 machine produces 1450/10 = 145 m of cloth.

At 95% efficiency, 4 machines produce 4•145•95/100 = 551 m of cloth.

At 90% efficiency, 6 machines produce 6•145•90/100 = 783 m of cloth.

Total cloth produced by all 10 machines = 551 + 783 = 1334 m

Since the information provided and the question are based on 8 hours, we did not need to use time to reach the answer.

16. D
Distance covered by the car = 60 X 3.5 = 210 km.
Time required by the motorbike = 210/40 = 5.25 hr.

17. C
Let the grandson's age be X and the grandfather's age be Y. According we have,
y = 8x
and
y + 6 = 5(x + 6)
Solving we get y = 64

18. B
5n + (19 – 2)) = 67, 5n + 17 = 67, 5n = 67 -17, 5n = 50, n = 50/5 = 10

19. C
The ratio between apples and oranges is 2 to 8 or 2:8. Bring

to the lowest terms by dividing both sides by 2 gives 1:4.

20. A
The ratio between black and blue pens is 7 to 28 or 7:28. Bring to the lowest terms by dividing both sides by 7 gives 1:4.

21. C
32 + 356 = 388. Therefore X + 388 = 920, X = 920 − 388 = 532

22. B
The ratio between green, red and blue candies is 3:12:9. Bring to the lowest terms by dividing the sides by 3 gives 1:4:3.

23. A
12 x 12 = 144, so 144/x =12, X = 12

24. A
34 x 2 = 68, so A − 68 = 18, A = 68 + 18 = 86

25. D
X% of 120 = 30, so X = 30/120 x 100/1 = 300/12 = 25

This questions can be estimated quickly just by looking at the numbers. 30 and 120 are related by, as 4 X 30 = 120. 4 expressed as a percent is 25%. Check quickly, 25% of 120 = 30.

26. B
X * 25% x 100 = 76, therefore, X * 4 = 76, X = 76/4 = 19

27. D
X% of 250 = 50, so X = 50/250 x 100/1= 100/5 = 20

28. D
Multiples of 3 are 3, 6, 9, 12 and Multiples of 4 are 4, 8, 12, Therefore the least common multiple is 12.

This can be estimated quickly. 3 is a prime number so the only possible multiples of 3 and any other number, say X, will be 3X.

29. C
The ratio between gold, silver and bronze coins is 2:6:8.
Bring to the lowest terms by dividing each side by 2 gives 1:3:4.

30. A
Multiples of 8 are 8, 16, 24 and multiples of 12 are 12, 24, 36, so the least common multiple is 24.

31. D
$3x = 20 + 7 = 27$, $x = 27/3$, $x = 9$.

32. C
Multiples of 2 are 2, 4, 6 and Multiples of 3 are 3, 6, so the least common is 6.

33. B
$124 = 12c - 20$, $124 + 20 = 12c$, $144 = 12c$, $c = 144/12 = 12$.

34. C
Add the whole numbers and then add the fractions, therefore $3 + 5 \{8/9 + 5/6\}$, then find a common denominator for the fractions $8 \{16/18 + 15/18\} = 8\ 31/18$, then simplify to $9\ 13/18$

35. D
Subtract the whole numbers and then subtract the fractions, therefore $7 - 2 \{4/5 - 2/5\}$, the fractions has a common denominator, so
$5 (4-2/5) = 5\ 2/5$.

36. A
Three plus a number times 7 equals 42. Let X be the number.
$(3 + X)$ times $7 = 42$
$7(3 + X) = 42$

37. C
$5205 / 25 = 208.20$ or, about 208.

38. D
Two parallel lines(m & side AB) intersected by side AC
$a = 50°$ (interior angles)

39. A
The wheel travels 2πr distance when it makes one revolution. Here, r stands for the radius. The radius is given as 25 cm in the figure. So,

2πr = 2π•25 = 50π cm is the distance travelled in one revolution.

In 175 revolutions: 175•50π = 8750π cm is travelled.

We are asked to find the distance in meter.

1 m = 100 cm So;

8750π cm = 8750π / 100 = 87.5π m

40. C
Equilateral triangle with 9 cm sides
Perimeter = 9+9+9
= 27 cm.

41. C
In the figure, we are given a large circle and a small circle inside it; with the diameter equal to the radius of the large one. The diameter of the small circle is 4 cm. This means that its radius is 2 cm. Since the diameter of the small circle is the radius of the large circle, the radius of the large circle is 4 cm. The area of a circle is calculated by: πr² where r is the radius.

Area of the small circle: π(2)² = 4π

Area of the large circle: π(4)² = 16π

The difference area is found by:

Area of the large circle - Area of the small circle = 16π - 4π = 12π

42. C
Volume of a cylinder is π x r² x h
Diameter = 5 ft. so radius is 2.5 ft.
Volume of the cylinder = π x 2.5² x 2
= π x 6.25 x 2 = 12.5 π
Approximate π to 3.142

Volume of the cylinder = 39.25

Volume of a rectangle = height X width X length.
= 5 X 5 X 4 = 100

Total volume = Volume of rectangular solid + volume of cylinder
Total volume = 100 + 39.25
Total volume = 139.25 ft^3 or approximately 140 ft^3

43. D
Two parallel lines intersected by a third line with angles of 75°
x = 75° (corresponding angles)
x + y = 180°(supplementary angles)
y = 180° - 75°
y = 105°

44. D
To find the total turnout in all three polling stations, we need to proportion the number of voters to the number of all registered voters.

Number of total voters = 945 + 860 + 1210 = 3015

Number of total registered voters = 1270 + 1050 + 1440 = 3760

Percentage turnout over all three polling stations = 3015•100/3760 = 80.19%

Checking the answers, we round 80.19 to the nearest whole number: 80%

45. C
Substitute the known terms, (3 x 2) + (4 x 4) x 8 =, 6 + 4 x 8=, 10 x 8 = 80

Practice Test Questions Set 2

THE QUESTIONS BELOW ARE NOT THE SAME AS YOU WILL FIND ON THE ISEE® - THAT WOULD BE TOO EASY! And nobody knows what the questions will be and they change all the time. Below are general questions that cover the same subject areas as the ISEE®. So, while the format and exact wording of the questions may differ slightly, and change from year to year, if you can answer the questions below, you will have no problem with the ISEE®.

For the best results, take these Practice Test Questions as if it were the real exam. Set aside time when you will not be disturbed, and a location that is quiet and free of distractions. Read the instructions carefully, read each question carefully, and answer to the best of your ability.
Use the bubble answer sheets provided. When you have completed the Practice Questions, check your answer against the Answer Key and read the explanation provided.

Do not attempt more than one set of practice test questions in one day. After completing the first practice test, wait two or three days before attempting the second set of questions.

Section I – Verbal Reasoning

Questions: 40
Time: 20 Minutes

Section II – Quantitative Reasoning

Questions: 35
Time: 35 Minutes

Section III – Reading Comprehension

Questions: 40
Time: 40 Minutes

Section IV – Mathematics

Questions: 45
Time: 40 Minutes

Verbal Reasoning

1. A B C D
2. A B C D
3. A B C D
4. A B C D
5. A B C D
6. A B C D
7. A B C D
8. A B C D
9. A B C D
10. A B C D
11. A B C D
12. A B C D
13. A B C D
14. A B C D
15. A B C D
16. A B C D
17. A B C D
18. A B C D
19. A B C D
20. A B C D
21. A B C D
22. A B C D
23. A B C D
24. A B C D
25. A B C D
26. A B C D
27. A B C D
28. A B C D
29. A B C D
30. A B C D
31. A B C D
32. A B C D
33. A B C D
34. A B C D
35. A B C D
36. A B C D
37. A B C D
38. A B C D
39. A B C D
40. A B C D

Quantitative Reasoning

1. Ⓐ Ⓑ Ⓒ Ⓓ
2. Ⓐ Ⓑ Ⓒ Ⓓ
3. Ⓐ Ⓑ Ⓒ Ⓓ
4. Ⓐ Ⓑ Ⓒ Ⓓ
5. Ⓐ Ⓑ Ⓒ Ⓓ
6. Ⓐ Ⓑ Ⓒ Ⓓ
7. Ⓐ Ⓑ Ⓒ Ⓓ
8. Ⓐ Ⓑ Ⓒ Ⓓ
9. Ⓐ Ⓑ Ⓒ Ⓓ
10. Ⓐ Ⓑ Ⓒ Ⓓ
11. Ⓐ Ⓑ Ⓒ Ⓓ
12. Ⓐ Ⓑ Ⓒ Ⓓ
13. Ⓐ Ⓑ Ⓒ Ⓓ
14. Ⓐ Ⓑ Ⓒ Ⓓ
15. Ⓐ Ⓑ Ⓒ Ⓓ
16. Ⓐ Ⓑ Ⓒ Ⓓ
17. Ⓐ Ⓑ Ⓒ Ⓓ
18. Ⓐ Ⓑ Ⓒ Ⓓ
19. Ⓐ Ⓑ Ⓒ Ⓓ
20. Ⓐ Ⓑ Ⓒ Ⓓ
21. Ⓐ Ⓑ Ⓒ Ⓓ
22. Ⓐ Ⓑ Ⓒ Ⓓ
23. Ⓐ Ⓑ Ⓒ Ⓓ
24. Ⓐ Ⓑ Ⓒ Ⓓ
25. Ⓐ Ⓑ Ⓒ Ⓓ
26. Ⓐ Ⓑ Ⓒ Ⓓ
27. Ⓐ Ⓑ Ⓒ Ⓓ
28. Ⓐ Ⓑ Ⓒ Ⓓ
29. Ⓐ Ⓑ Ⓒ Ⓓ
30. Ⓐ Ⓑ Ⓒ Ⓓ
31. Ⓐ Ⓑ Ⓒ Ⓓ
32. Ⓐ Ⓑ Ⓒ Ⓓ
33. Ⓐ Ⓑ Ⓒ Ⓓ
34. Ⓐ Ⓑ Ⓒ Ⓓ
35. Ⓐ Ⓑ Ⓒ Ⓓ

Reading Comprehension

1. A B C D
2. A B C D
3. A B C D
4. A B C D
5. A B C D
6. A B C D
7. A B C D
8. A B C D
9. A B C D
10. A B C D
11. A B C D
12. A B C D
13. A B C D
14. A B C D
15. A B C D
16. A B C D
17. A B C D
18. A B C D
19. A B C D
20. A B C D
21. A B C D
22. A B C D
23. A B C D
24. A B C D
25. A B C D
26. A B C D
27. A B C D
28. A B C D
29. A B C D
30. A B C D
31. A B C D
32. A B C D
33. A B C D
34. A B C D
35. A B C D
36. A B C D
37. A B C D
38. A B C D
39. A B C D
40. A B C D

Mathematics

1. A B C D
2. A B C D
3. A B C D
4. A B C D
5. A B C D
6. A B C D
7. A B C D
8. A B C D
9. A B C D
10. A B C D
11. A B C D
12. A B C D
13. A B C D
14. A B C D
15. A B C D
16. A B C D
17. A B C D
18. A B C D
19. A B C D
20. A B C D
21. A B C D
22. A B C D
23. A B C D
24. A B C D
25. A B C D
26. A B C D
27. A B C D
28. A B C D
29. A B C D
30. A B C D
31. A B C D
32. A B C D
33. A B C D
34. A B C D
35. A B C D
36. A B C D
37. A B C D
38. A B C D
39. A B C D
40. A B C D
41. A B C D
42. A B C D
43. A B C D
44. A B C D
45. A B C D
46. A B C D
47. A B C D
48. A B C D
49. A B C D
50. A B C D

Section I – Verbal Reasoning

1. COMPETENT

    a. Pensive

    b. Able

    c. Allow

    d. Honest

2. ANTIDOTE

    a. Cure

    b. Lure

    c. Craft

    d. Affiliation

3. CONSENSUS

    a. Quality

    b. Compensation

    c. Agreement

    d. Command

4. MAGNIFY

    a. Amplify

    b. Trace

    c. Shade

    d. Agility

5. IMMACULATE

   a. Haphazard
   b. Perfect
   c. Clean
   d. Payment

6. VIABLE

   a. Haste
   b. Complete
   c. Feasible
   d. Exceptional

7. RATIONALE

   a. Deduct
   b. Reason
   c. Congenial
   d. Errant

8. TINGE

   a. Touch
   b. Spot
   c. Slur
   d. Rant

9. GIST

   a. Context
   b. Flourish
   c. Summary
   d. Speculation

10. INSTIGATE

a. Correct
b. Solute
c. Initiate
d. Lament

11. EXPERTISE

a. Specialty
b. Institutionalize
c. Accentuate
d. Brazen

12. FERTILE

a. Fruitful
b. Vacant
c. Overstuffed
d. Poor

13. ROWDY

a. Noisy
b. Rich
c. Ancient
d. Crazy

14. COURTEOUS

a. Polite
b. Exceptional
c. Loving
d. Loyal

15. LEAN

    a. Thin

    b. Straight

    c. Lazy

    d. Blank

16. AUDACIOUS

    a. Bored

    b. Daring

    c. Flighty

    d. Outrageous

17. CONSTITUTE

    a. Establish

    b. Inaugurate

    c. Accomplish

    d. Embellish

18. CORRUPT

    a. Unscrupulous

    b. Ethical

    c. Unimaginable

    d. Impregnable

19. DISPENSE

    a. Distribute

    b. Annoy

    c. Collect

    d. Advise

20. DURATION

    a. Speed

    b. Length

    c. Width

    d. Height

Fill in the blank.

21. Her _____ talent wowed the audience during the contest.

    a. Ugly

    b. Extraordinary

    c. Plain

    d. Ordinary

22. Jean was _____ when her little brother destroyed her favorite doll.

    a. Happy

    b. Lonely

    c. Angry

    d. Surprised

23. We will _____ about our scores on the pop quiz.

    a. Ask

    b. Complain

    c. Suggest

    d. Command

24. The car accident was an/a _____ experience the victims want to forget.

    a. Terrible

    b. Pleasant

    c. Wonderful

    d. Unforgettable

25. Cinderella's _____ stepmother failed in the end.

    a. Understanding

    b. Happy

    c. Evil

    d. Supportive

26. Her business success showed that she was very _____.

    a. Slow

    b. Astute

    c. Ignorant

    d. Heinous

27. It is boring and I would rather not go, but the ceremony is _____.

    a. Mandatory

    b. Optional

    c. Adaptable

    d. None of the above.

28. We don't want to hear the whole thing. Just the _____ facts please.

   a. Irrelevant

   b. Erroneous

   c. Relevant

   d. Trivial

29. She works in a cubicle answering the phone all day. Her doctor says she is too _____.

   a. Sedentary

   b. Active

   c. Morbid

   d. None of the Above.

30. I don't know why he is being so nice. I am sure he has a/an _____ motive.

   a. Inferior

   b. Ulterior

   c. Simplistic

   d. Unfortunate

31. We cannot reveal the source. It was posted by _____.

   a. Anonymous

   b. Author

   c. Someone

   d. Nobody

32. I have never seen anyone so rude. His behavior was _____.

    a. Monstrous
    b. Perfect
    c. Atrocious
    d. Suspicious

33. I see that sign everywhere. It is much more _____ than I thought.

    a. Prelude
    b. Prevalent
    c. Ratify
    d. Rational

34. Her attitude was very _____.

    a. Idle
    b. Nonchalant
    c. Portly
    d. Portend

35. The water in the pond has been sitting for so long it is _____.

    a. Stagnant
    b. Sediment
    c. Stupor
    d. Residue

36. I cannot wait to try some of the _____ dishes served in the new restaurant.

   a. Succor
   b. Expensive
   c. Variable
   d. Delicious

37. Can you _____ the character of Juliet in the play?

   a. Report
   b. Describe
   c. State
   d. Draw

38. The soldiers _____ the rebel's camp.

   a. Ruined
   b. Ended
   c. Fixed
   d. Conquered

39. There is a big _____ in Esther and Pete's grades.

   a. Complication
   b. Dissimilarity
   c. Minus
   d. Increase

40. I can _____ my goals in life when I study hard.

   a. Finish
   b. Forget
   c. Effect
   d. Achieve

Section II – Quantitative Reasoning

1. Simplify 6 3/5 – 4 4/5

    a. 2 4/5
    b. 2 3/5
    c. 2 9/5
    d. 1 1/5

2. Estimate 46,227 + 101,032.

    a. 14,700
    b. 147,000
    c. 14,700,000
    d. 104,700

3. Solve $\sqrt{121}$

    a. 11
    b. 12
    c. 21
    d. None of the above

4. Kate's father is 32 years older than Kate is. In 5 years, he will be five times older. How old is Kate?

    a. 2
    b. 3
    c. 5
    d. 6

5. If Lynn can type a page in p minutes, what portion of the page can she do in 5 minutes?

    a. 5/p
    b. p - 5
    c. p + 5
    d. p/5

6. If Sally can paint a house in 4 hours, and John can paint the same house in 6 hours, how long will it take for both of them to paint the house together?

    a. 2 hours and 24 minutes
    b. 3 hours and 12 minutes
    c. 3 hours and 44 minutes
    d. 4 hours and 10 minutes

7. Sales of a local football team's season tickets have gone up 10% in the current season to 880 tickets. Last year, they sold X season tickets. X equals:

    a. 700
    b. 800
    c. 880
    d. 928

8. In an office, 12 employees can finish a task in 7 hours. If two of them are absent, how much more time will they have to work to complete the task?

    a. 10 minutes
    b. 12 minutes
    c. 15 minutes
    d. 20 minutes

9. A bullet train traveling at 300km/hr passes station A at 8:56 pm. What time will the train reach station B, which is 45km away?

    a. 9:03 pm
    b. 9:05 pm
    c. 9:07 pm
    d. 9:10 pm

10. There were some oranges in a basket, by adding 8/5 of these the total became 130. How many oranges were in the basket before?

    a. 60
    b. 50
    c. 40
    d. 35

11. In a 30-minute test, there are 40 problems. A student solved 28 problems in first 25 minutes. How many seconds should she give to each of the remaining problems?

    a. 20 seconds
    b. 23 seconds
    c. 25 seconds
    d. 27 seconds

12. 2/3 of what number added to 10 is 3 times 15?

    a. 50
    b. 52.5
    c. 65
    d. 72.8

13. What number is 25 more than 1/3 of 27?

　　a. 34
　　b. -16
　　c. 20
　　d. 18

14. Richard sold 12 shirts for total revenue of $336 at 8% profit. What is the purchase price of each shirt?

　　a. $25.75
　　b. $24.50
　　c. $23.75
　　d. $22.50

15. If we know it takes 12 men to operate four machines, how many are required to operate 20 machines?

　　a. 6
　　b. 20
　　c. 60
　　d. 9

16. What number is 10 less than 5 squared?

　　a. 25
　　b. 10
　　c. 15
　　d. 40

17. What number divided by 5 is 2/3 of 100?

　　a. 333.33
　　b. 444.44
　　c. 250
　　d. 100

18.

Column A	Column B
.97 - .49	.76 + .21

a. Column A is greater
b. Column B is greater
c. The quantities are equal
d. The relationship cannot be determined

19.

Column A	Column B
1/3 + 1/5 + 3/6	2/3 + 3/4

a. Column A is greater
b. Column B is greater
c. The quantities are equal
d. The relationship cannot be determined

20.

Column A	Column B
2/8 + 5/6	6/8 + 4/2

a. Column A is greater
b. Column B is greater
c. The quantities are equal
d. The relationship cannot be determined

21.

Column A	Column B
Martin's taxes	$290

Martin earns $1800 per month and pays 16% taxes.

    a. Column A is greater
    b. Column B is greater
    c. The quantities are equal
    d. The relationship cannot be determined

22.

Column A	Column B
The area of a square with 5 cm. sides	The area of a rectangle with sides 2 cm and 10 cm.

    a. Column A is greater
    b. Column B is greater
    c. The quantities are equal
    d. The relationship cannot be determined

23.

Column A	Column B
The area of a circle with 19 cm. radius	The area of a square with 25 cm sides

    a. Column A is greater
    b. Column B is greater
    c. The quantities are equal
    d. The relationship cannot be determined

24.

Column A	Column B
The area of a circle with 9 cm. radius	The area of a triangle with 5 cm base and 10 cm height

a. Column A is greater
b. Column B is greater
c. The quantities are equal
d. The relationship cannot be determined

25.

Column A	Column B
40% of 500	12% of 1350

a. Column A is greater
b. Column B is greater
c. The quantities are equal
d. The relationship cannot be determined

26.

Column A	Column B
18% of 150	22% of 60

a. Column A is greater
b. Column B is greater
c. The quantities are equal
d. The relationship cannot be determined

27.

Column A	Column B
15% of 50	12% of 75

a. Column A is greater
b. Column B is greater
c. The quantities are equal
d. The relationship cannot be determined

28.

Column A	Column B
.234 + .673	.990 - .378

a. Column A is greater
b. Column B is greater
c. The quantities are equal
d. The relationship cannot be determined

29.

Column A	Column B
Probability of drawing a red ball.	Probability of drawing a yellow ball.

There are 6 red balls and 4 yellow balls in a box.

    a. Column A is greater

    b. Column B is greater

    c. The quantities are equal

    d. The relationship cannot be determined

30.

Column A	Column B
Probability of drawing a red ball.	Probability of drawing a green ball.

There are 6 red balls, 5 green balls and 4 yellow balls in a box.

    a. Column A is greater

    b. Column B is greater

    c. The quantities are equal

    d. The relationship cannot be determined

31.

Column A	Column B
Cost of John's sweater.	Cost of Jill's Jacket

Jack bought a $75 sweater at 22% off and Jill bought a $100 jacket at 35% off.

    a. Column A is greater
    b. Column B is greater
    c. The quantities are equal
    d. The relationship cannot be determined

32.

Column A	Column B
2/5	.993 - .34

    a. Column A is greater
    b. Column B is greater
    c. The quantities are equal
    d. The relationship cannot be determined

33.

Column A	Column B
1/3 + 4/7	6.93 - 6.34

    a. Column A is greater
    b. Column B is greater
    c. The quantities are equal
    d. The relationship cannot be determined

34.

Column A	Column B
.25 + .67	.89 - .34

    a. Column A is greater
    b. Column B is greater
    c. The quantities are equal
    d. The relationship cannot be determined

35.

Column A	Column B
.13 + .64	.62 - .14

    a. Column A is greater
    b. Column B is greater
    c. The quantities are equal
    d. The relationship cannot be determined

Section III - Reading

Questions 1-4 refer to the following passage.

Passage 1 - The Respiratory System

The respiratory system's function is to allow oxygen exchange through all parts of the body. The anatomy or structure of the exchange system, and the uses of the exchanged gases, varies depending on the organism. In humans and other mammals, for example, the anatomical features of the respiratory system include airways, lungs, and the respiratory muscles. Molecules of oxygen and carbon dioxide are passively exchanged, by diffusion, between the gaseous external environment and the blood. This exchange process occurs in the alveolar region of the lungs.

Other animals, such as insects, have respiratory systems with very simple anatomical features, and in amphibians even the skin plays a vital role in gas exchange. Plants also have respiratory systems but the direction of gas exchange can be opposite to that of animals.

The respiratory system can also be divided into physiological, or functional, zones. These include the conducting zone (the region for gas transport from the outside atmosphere to just above the alveoli), the transitional zone, and the respiratory zone (the alveolar region where gas exchange occurs). [9]

1. What can we infer from the first paragraph in this passage?

    a. Human and mammal respiratory systems are the same.

    b. The lungs are an important part of the respiratory system.

    c. The respiratory system varies in different mammals.

    d. Oxygen and carbon dioxide are passive exchanged by the respiratory system.

2. What is the process by which molecules of oxygen and carbon dioxide are passively exchanged?

    a. Transfusion
    b. Affusion
    c. Diffusion
    d. Respiratory confusion

3. What organ plays an important role in gas exchange in amphibians?

    a. The skin
    b. The lungs
    c. The gills
    d. The mouth

4. What are the three physiological zones of the respiratory system?

    a. Conducting, transitional, respiratory zones
    b. Redacting, transitional, circulatory zones
    c. Conducting, circulatory, inhibiting zones
    d. Transitional, inhibiting, conducting zones

Questions 5 - 8 refer to the following passage.

ABC Electric Warranty

ABC Electric Company warrants that its products are free from defects in material and workmanship. Subject to the conditions and limitations set forth below, ABC Electric will, at its option, either repair or replace any part of its products that prove defective due to improper workmanship or materials.

This limited warranty does not cover any damage to the product from improper installation, accident, abuse, misuse, natural disaster, insufficient or excessive electrical supply, abnormal mechanical or environmental conditions, or any unauthorized disassembly, repair, or modification.

This limited warranty also does not apply to any product on which the original identification information has been altered, or removed, has not been handled or packaged correctly, or has been sold as second-hand.

This limited warranty covers only repair, replacement, refund or credit for defective ABC Electric products, as provided above.

5. I tried to repair my ABC Electric blender, but could not, so can I get it repaired under this warranty?

    a. Yes, the warranty still covers the blender.

    b. No, the warranty does not cover the blender.

    c. Uncertain. ABC Electric may or may not cover repairs under this warranty.

6. My ABC Electric fan is not working. Will ABC Electric provide a new one or repair this one?

    a. ABC Electric will repair my fan

    b. ABC Electric will replace my fan

    c. ABC Electric could either replace or repair my fan or I can request either a replacement or a repair.

7. My stove was damaged in a flood. Does this warranty cover my stove?

    a. Yes, it is covered.

    b. No, it is not covered.

    c. It may or may not be covered.

    d. ABC Electric will decide if it is covered.

8. Which of the following is an example of improper workmanship?

    a. Missing parts

    b. Defective parts

    c. Scratches on the front

    d. None of the above

Questions 9 – 11 refer to the following passage.

Passage 2 – Mythology

The main characters in myths are usually gods or supernatural heroes. As sacred stories, rulers and priests have traditionally endorsed their myths and as a result, myths have a close link with religion and politics. In the society where a myth originates, the natives believe the myth is a true account of the remote past. In fact, many societies have two categories of traditional narrative—(1) "true stories," or myths, and (2) "false stories," or fables.

Myths generally take place during a primordial age, when the world was still young, before achieving its current form. These stories explain how the world gained its current form and why the culture developed its customs, institutions, and taboos. Closely related to myth are legend and folktale. Myths, legends, and folktales are different types of traditional stories. Unlike myths, folktales can take place at any time and any place, and the natives do not usually consider them true or sacred. Legends, on the other hand, are similar to myths in that many people have traditionally considered them true. Legends take place in a more recent time, when the world was much as it is today. In addition, legends generally feature humans as their main characters, whereas myths have superhuman characters. [7]

9. We can infer from this passage that

a. Folktales took place in a time far past, before civilization covered the earth.

b. Humankind uses myth to explain how the world was created.

c. Myths revolve around gods or supernatural beings; the local community usually accepts these stories as not true.

d. The only difference between a myth and a legend is the time setting of the story.

10. The main purpose of this passage is

a. To distinguish between many types of traditional stories, and explain the background of some traditional story categories.

b. To determine whether myths and legends might be true accounts of history.

c. To show the importance of folktales how these traditional stories made life more bearable in harder times.

d. None of the Above.

11. How are folktales different from myths?

a. Folktales and myth are the same.

b. Folktales are not true and generally not sacred and take place anytime.

c. Myths are not true and generally not sacred and take place anytime.

d. Folktales explained the formation of the world and myths do not.

Getting Started

    A Better Score Is Possible 6
    Types of Multiple Choice 9
    Multiple Choice Step-by-Step 12
    Tips for Reading the Instructions 13
    General Multiple Choice Tips 14
    Multiple Choice Strategy Practice 20
    Answer Key 39

12. Based on the partial Table of Contents above, what is this book about?

    a. How to answer multiple choice questions

    b. Different types of multiple choice questions

    c. How to write a test

    d. None of the above

Questions 13-16 refer to the following passage.

Passage 3 – Myths, Legend and Folklore

Cultural historians draw a distinction between myth, legend and folktale simply as a way to group traditional stories. However, in many cultures, drawing a sharp line between myths and legends is not that simple. Instead of dividing their traditional stories into myths, legends, and folktales, some cultures divide them into two categories. The first category roughly corresponds to folktales, and the second is one that combines myths and legends. Similarly, we can not always separate myths from folktales. One society might consider a story true, making it a myth. Another society may believe the story is fiction, which makes it a folktale. In fact, when a myth loses its status as part of a religious system, it often takes on traits more typical of folktales, with its formerly divine characters now appearing as human heroes, giants, or fairies. Myth, legend, and folktale are only a few of the categories of traditional stories. Other categories include anecdotes and some kinds of jokes. Traditional stories, in turn, are only one category within the larger category of folklore, which also includes items such as gestures, costumes, and music. [7]

13. The main idea of this passage is that

a. Myths, fables, and folktales are not the same thing, and each describes a specific type of story.

b. Traditional stories can be categorized in different ways by different people.

c. Cultures use myths for religious purposes, and when this is no longer true, the people forget and discard these myths.

d. Myths can never become folk tales, because one is true, and the other is false.

14. The terms myth and legend are

a. Categories that are synonymous with true and false.

b. Categories that group traditional stories according to certain characteristics.

c. Interchangeable, because both terms mean a story that is passed down from generation to generation.

d. Meant to distinguish between a story that involves a hero and a cultural message and a story meant only to entertain.

15. Traditional story categories not only include myths and legends, but

a. Can also include gestures, since some cultures passed these down before the written and spoken word.

b. In addition, folklore refers to stories involving fables and fairy tales.

c. These story categories can also include folk music and traditional dress.

d. Traditional stories themselves are a part of the larger category of folklore, which may also include costumes, gestures, and music.

16. This passage shows that

  a. There is a distinct difference between a myth and a legend, although both are folktales.

  b. Myths are folktales, but folktales are not myths.

  c. Myths, legends, and folktales play an important part in tradition and the past, and are a rich and colorful part of history.

  d. Most cultures consider myths to be true.

Questions 17 - 21 refer to the following passage.

Passage 4 – Trees I

Trees are an important part of the natural landscape because they prevent erosion and protect ecosystems in and under their branches. Trees also play an important role in producing oxygen and reducing carbon dioxide in the atmosphere, as well as moderating ground temperatures. Trees are important elements in landscaping and agriculture, both for their visual appeal and for their crops, such as apples, and other fruit. Wood from trees is a building material, and a primary energy source in many developing countries. Trees also play a role in many of the world's mythologies. [8]

17. What are two reasons trees are important in the natural landscape?

  a. They prevent erosion and produce oxygen.

  b. They produce fruit and are important elements in landscaping.

  c. Trees are not important in the natural landscape.

  d. Trees produce carbon dioxide and prevent erosion.

18. What kind of ecosystems do trees protect?

   a. Trees do not protect ecosystems.

   b. Weather sheltered ecosystems.

   c. Ecosystems around the base and under the branches.

   d. All of the above.

19. Which of the following is true?

   a. Trees provide a primary food source in the developing world.

   b. Trees provide a primary building material in the developing world.

   c. Trees provide a primary energy source in the developing world.

   d. Trees provide a primary oxygen source in the developing world.

20. Why are trees important for agriculture?

   a. Because of their crops.

   b. Because they shelter ecosystems.

   c. Because they are a source of energy.

   d. Because of their visual appeal.

21. What do trees do to the atmosphere?

   a. Trees produce carbon dioxide and reduce oxygen.

   b. Trees product oxygen and carbon dioxide.

   c. Trees reduce oxygen and carbon dioxide.

   d. Trees produce oxygen and reduce carbon dioxide.

Questions 22 - 25 refer to the following passage.

Passage 5 Women and Advertising

Only in the last few generations have media messages been so widespread and so readily seen, heard, and read by so many people. Advertising is an important part of both selling and buying anything from soap to cereal to jeans. For whatever reason, more consumers are women than are men. Media message are subtle but powerful, and more attention has been paid lately to how these message affect women.

Of all the products that women buy, makeup, clothes, and other stylistic or cosmetic products are among the most popular. This means that companies focus their advertising on women, promising them that their product will make her feel, look, or smell better than the next company's product will. This competition has resulted in advertising that is more and more ideal and less and less possible for everyday women. However, because women do look to these ideals and the products they represent as how they can potentially become, many women have developed unhealthy attitudes about themselves when they have failed to become those ideals.

In recent years, more companies have tried to change advertisements to be healthier for women. This includes featuring models of more sizes and addressing a huge outcry against unfair tools such as airbrushing and photo editing. There is debate about what the right balance between real and ideal is, because fashion is also considered art and some changes are made to purposefully elevate fashionable products and signify that they are creative, innovative, and the work of individual people. Artists want their freedom protected as much as women do, and advertising agencies are often caught in the middle.

Some claim that the companies who make these changes are not doing enough. Many people worry that there are still not enough models of different sizes and different ethnicities. Some people claim that companies use this healthier type of advertisement not for the good of women, but because they would like to sell products to the women who are looking for these kinds of messages. This is also a hard balance to find: companies do need to make money, and women do need to feel respected.

While the focus of this change has been on women, advertising can also affect men, and this change will hopefully be a lesson on media for all consumers.

22. The second paragraph states that advertising focuses on women

    a. to shape what the ideal should be.

    b. because women buy makeup.

    c. because women are easily persuaded.

    d. because of the types of products that women buy.

23. According to the passage, fashion artists and female consumers are at odds because

    a. there is a debate going on and disagreement drives people apart.

    b. both of them are trying to protect their freedom to do something.

    c. artists want to elevate their products above the reach of women.

    d. women are creative, innovative, individual people.

24. The author uses the phrase "for whatever reason" in this passage to

    a. keep the focus of the paragraph on media messages and not on the differences between men and women

    b. show that the reason for this is unimportant

    c. argue that it is stupid that more women are consumers than men

    d. show that he or she is tired of talking about why media messages are important

25. This passage suggests that

    a. advertising companies are still working on making their messages better

    b. all advertising companies seek to be more approachable for women

    c. women are only buying from companies that respect them

    d. artists could stop producing fashionable products if they feel bullied

Questions 26 - 28 refer to the following passage.

Lowest Price Guarantee

Get it for less. Guaranteed!

ABC Electric will beat any advertised price by 10% of the difference.

    1) If you find a lower advertised price, we will beat it by 10% of the difference.

    2) If you find a lower advertised price within 30 days* of your purchase we will beat it by 10% of the difference.

    3) If our own price is reduced within 30 days* of your purchase, bring in your receipt and we will refund the difference.

*14 days for computers, monitors, printers, laptops, tablets, cellular & wireless devices, home security products, projectors, camcorders, digital cameras, radar detectors, portable DVD players, DJ and pro-audio equipment, and air conditioners.

26. I bought a radar detector 15 days ago and saw an ad for the same model only cheaper. Can I get 10% of the difference refunded?

    a. Yes. Since it is less than 30 days, you can get 10% of the difference refunded.

    b. No. Since it is more than 14 days, you cannot get 10% of the difference re-funded.

    c. It depends on the cashier.

    d. Yes. You can get the difference refunded.

27. I bought a flat-screen TV for $500 10 days ago and found an advertisement for the same TV, at another store, on sale for $400. How much will ABC refund under this guarantee?

    a. $100

    b. $110

    c. $10

    d. $400

28. What is the purpose of this passage?

    a. To inform

    b. To educate

    c. To persuade

    d. To entertain

Questions 29 - 32 refer to the following passage.

Passage 6 - Insects

Insects have segmented bodies supported by an exoskeleton, a hard outer covering made mostly of chitin. The segments of the body are organized into three distinctive connected units, a head, a thorax, and an abdomen. The head supports a pair of antennae, a pair of compound eyes, and three sets of appendages that form the mouthparts.

The thorax has six segmented legs and, if present in the species, two or four wings. The abdomen consists of eleven segments, though in a few species these segments may be fused together or very small.

Overall, there are 24 segments. The abdomen also contains most of the digestive, respiratory, excretory and reproductive internal structures. There is considerable variation and many adaptations in the body parts of insects especially wings, legs, antenna and mouthparts. [9]

29. How many units do insects have?

    a. Insects are divided into 24 units.

    b. Insects are divided into 3 units.

    c. Insects are divided into segments not units.

    d. It depends on the species.

30. Which of the following is true?

    a. All insects have 2 wings.

    b. All insects have 4 wings.

    c. Some insects have 2 wings.

    d. Some insects have 2 or 4 wings.

31. What is true of insect's abdomen?

    a. It contains some of the organs.

    b. It is too small for any organs.

    c. It contains all of the organs.

    d. None of the above.

32. Choose the best summary statement of this passage

a. This passage is about the physical characteristics of insects.
b. This passage is about insects.
c. This passage is about insects with exoskeletons.
d. None of the Above.

Questions 33 - 36 refer to the following passage.

Passage 7 - The Circulatory System

The circulatory system is an organ system that passes nutrients (such as amino acids and electrolytes), gases, hormones, and blood cells to and from cells in the body to help fight diseases and help stabilize body temperature and pH levels.

The circulatory system may be seen strictly as a blood distribution network, but some consider the circulatory system as composed of the cardiovascular system, which distributes blood, and the lymphatic system, which distributes lymph. While humans, as well as other vertebrates, have a closed cardiovascular system (meaning that the blood never leaves the network of arteries, veins and capillaries), some invertebrate groups have an open cardiovascular system. The most primitive animal phyla lack circulatory systems. The lymphatic system, on the other hand, is an open system.

Two types of fluids move through the circulatory system: blood and lymph. The blood, heart, and blood vessels form the cardiovascular system. The lymph, the lymph nodes, and lymph vessels form the lymphatic system. The cardiovascular system and the lymphatic system collectively make up the circulatory system.

The main components of the human cardiovascular system are the heart and the blood vessels. It includes: the pulmonary circulation, a "loop" through the lungs where blood is oxygenated; and the systemic circulation, a "loop" through the rest of the body to provide oxygenated blood. An average adult contains five to six quarts (roughly 4.7 to 5.7 liters) of blood, which consists of plasma, red blood cells, white blood cells, and platelets. Also, the digestive system works with the circulatory system to provide the nutrients the system needs to keep the heart pumping. [10]

33. What can we infer from the first paragraph?

    a. An important purpose of the circulatory system is that of fighting diseases.

    b. The most important function of the circulatory system is to give the person energy.

    c. The least important function of the circulatory system is that of growing skin cells.

    d. The entire purpose of the circulatory system is not known.

34. Do humans have an open or closed circulatory system?

    a. Open

    b. Closed

    c. Usually open, though sometimes closed

    d. Usually closed, though sometimes open

35. In addition to blood, what two components form the cardiovascular system?

    a. The heart and the lungs

    b. The lungs and the veins

    c. The heart and the blood vessels

    d. The blood vessels and the nerves

36. Which system, along with the circulatory system, helps provide nutrients to keep the human heart pumping?

    a. The skeletal system

    b. The digestive system

    c. The immune system

    d. The nervous system

Questions 37 - 40 refer to the following passage.

Passage 8 FDR, the Treaty of Versailles, and the Fourteen Points

At the conclusion of World War I, both those who had won the war and those who were forced to admit defeat welcomed the end of the war and anticipated that a peace treaty would be signed. The American president, Franklin D. Roosevelt, played an important part in proposing what the agreements should be and did so through his Fourteen Points.

World War I had begun in 1914 when an Austrian archduke was assassinated, leading to a domino effect that pulled the world's most powerful countries into war on a large scale. The war catalyzed the creation and use of deadly weapons that had not previously existed, resulting in a great loss of soldiers on both sides of the fighting. More than 9 million soldiers were killed.

The United States agreed to enter the war right before it ended, and they believed that its decision to become finally involved brought on the end of the war. FDR made it very clear that the U.S. was entering the war for moral reasons and had an agenda focused on world peace. The Fourteen Points were individual goals and ideas (focused on peace, free trade, open communication, and self reliance) that FDR wanted the power nations to strive for now that the war had concluded. He was optimistic and had many ideas about what could be accomplished through and during the post-war peace. However, FDR's fourteen points were poorly received when he presented them to the leaders of other world powers, many of whom wanted only to help their own countries and to punish the Germans for fueling the war, and they fell by the wayside. World War II was imminent, for Germany lost everything.

Some historians believe that the other leaders who participated in the Treaty of Versailles weren't receptive to the Fourteen Points because World War I was fought almost entirely on European soil, and the United States lost much less than did the other powers. FDR was in a unique position to determine the fate of the war, but doing it on his own terms did not help accomplish his goals. This is only one historical example of how the United State has tried to use its power as an important country, but found itself limited because of geological or ideological factors.

37. The main idea of this passage is that

    a. World War I was unfair because no fighting took place in America.

    b. World War II happened because of the Treaty of Versailles.

    c. the power the United States has to help other countries also prevents it from helping other countries.

    d. Franklin D. Roosevelt was one of the United States' smartest presidents.

38. According to the second paragraph, World War I started because

    a. an archduke was assassinated.

    b. weapons that were more deadly had been developed.

    c. a domino effect of allies agreeing to help each other.

    d. the world's most powerful countries were large.

39. The author includes the detail that 9 million soldiers were killed

   a. to demonstrate why European leaders were hesitant to accept peace.

   b. to show the reader the dangers of deadly weapons.

   c. to make the reader think about which countries lost the most soldiers.

   d. to demonstrate why World War II was imminent.

40. According to this passage, it can be understood that the word catalyzed means

   a. analyzed

   b. sped up

   c. invented

   d. funded

Section IV – Math

1. The sum of the digits of a 2-digit number is 12. If we switch the digits, the number we get will be greater than the initial one by 36. Find the initial number.

   a. 39

   b. 48

   c. 57

   d. 75

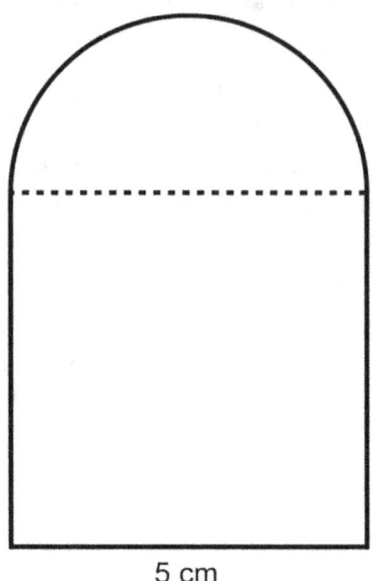

5 cm

Note: figure not drawn to scale

2. What is the perimeter of the above shape?

    a. 17.5 π cm
    b. 20 π cm
    c. 15 π cm
    d. 25 π cm

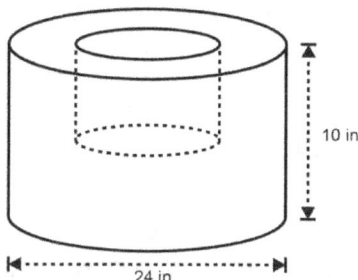

Note: figure not drawn to scale

3. What is the volume of the above solid made by a hollow cylinder that is half the size (in all dimensions) of the larger cylinder?

    a. 1440 π in³
    b. 1260 π in³
    c. 1040 π in³
    d. 960 π in³

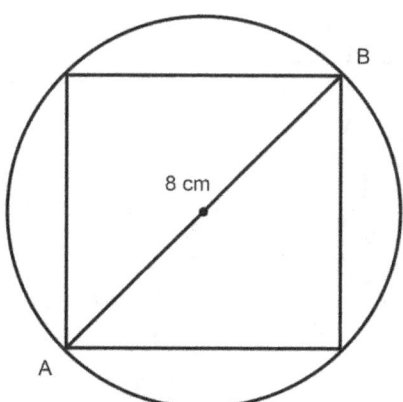

Note: figure not drawn to scale

4. What is area of the circle?

    a. 4 π cm²

    b. 12 π cm²

    c. 10 π cm²

    d. 16 π cm²

5. John jogs around a 75-meter diameter track 7 times. How much linear distance did he cover?

    a. 1250 meters

    b. 1450 meters

    c. 1650 meters

    d. 1725 meters

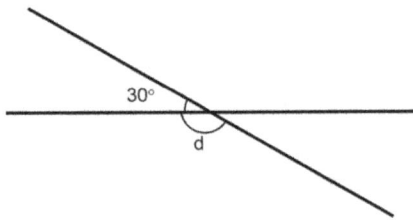

6. What is the indicated angle above?

    a. 150°

    b. 330°

    c. 60°

    d. 120°

7. On a circular jogging track with a circumference of 1.2 km, John, Tony and David walk at the rate of 120, 100 and 75 meters per minute respectively. If they all start walking in the same direction, how long will it take until they are together again?

    a. 200 minutes

    b. 220 minutes

    c. 240 minutes

    d. 260 minutes

8. On a scaled map, city A is 12.4 cm away from city B. If the scale is 1 cm = 5 km then what is the actual distance between these two cities?

    a. 12.4 km

    b. 48.4 km

    c. 58 km

    d. 62 km

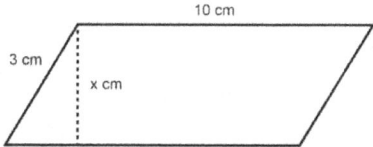

Note: figure not drawn to scale

9. What is the perimeter of the parallelogram above?

    a. 12 cm

    b. 26 cm

    c. 13 cm

    d. (13+x) cm

10. Estimate 2009 x 108.

    a. 110,000

    b. 2,0000

    c. 21,000

    d. 210,000

11. The playing times for three songs on a compact disc are as follows: 4 minutes 56 seconds for song A, 2 minutes 30 seconds for song B, 10 minutes 16 seconds for song C. What is the average playing time for the three songs?

    a. 17 minutes 42 seconds

    b. 6 minutes 7 seconds

    c. 6 minutes

    d. 5 minutes 54 seconds

12. John is a barber and receives 40% of the amount paid by his customers, and all of the tips. If a customer pays $8.50 for a haircut and leaves a tip of $1.30, how much money does John receive?

    a. $3.92

    b. $4.70

    c. $5.30

    d. $6.40

13. The length of a rectangle is 5 in. more than its width. The perimeter of the rectangle is 26 in. What is the width and length of the rectangle?

    a. Width 6 in., Length 9 in.

    b. Width 4 in., Length 9 in.

    c. Width 4 in., Length 5 in.

    d. Width 6 in., Length 11 in.

14. Calculate (3a + 4b) * d when A = 2, b = 4 and d = 8

    a. 40
    b. 150
    c. 112
    d. 176

15. c = 4, n = 5 and x = 3. Calculate 2cnx/2n

    a. 12
    b. 50
    c. 8
    d. 21

16. Simplify 3 1/2 / 2 4/5

    a. 1 1/4
    b. 2 1/4
    c. 1 1/3
    d. 2 1/3

17. Solve 2b/3 + 3a/5 − 2, where b = 9 and a = 10

    a. 5
    b. 10
    c. 20
    d. 9

18. Simplify (1/3 + 2/6) - (3/4 - 1/3)

    a. 1/4
    b. 5/11
    c. 3/7
    d. 2/9

19. Simplify (4/5 - 3/10) + (2/3 – 3/9) =

    a. 4/11
    b. 2/15
    c. 7/15
    d. 9/11

20. Translate the following into an equation: 2 + a number divided by 7.

    a. (2 + X)/7
    b. (7 + X)/2
    c. (2 + 7)/X
    d. 2/(7 + X)

21. If a = 12 and b = 8, solve 6b - a + 2a

    a. 12/9
    b. 18
    c. 16
    d. 12

22. Simplify 3 2/3 - 1 2/8

    a. 3/5
    b. 3/5
    c. 2 5/12
    d. 1 5/12

23. Simplify 7 2/5 – 4 3/10

    a. 3 1/10
    b. 3 2/5
    c. 4 1/5
    d. 3 7/10

24. Solve for x. -4 – 5x = 8x + 8

    a. 6
    b. 3
    c. 4
    d. 2

25. Solve 2 1/3 x 1 3/7 x 3/4

    a. 2 1/2
    b. 9
    c. 3 2/3
    d. 2 2/5

26. Simplify 7 4/5 – 4 2/3

    a. 4 2/5
    b. 3 2/15
    c. 3 7/15
    d. 4 3/5

27. Solve for x. 12x - 8 = 3x + 10

    a. 6
    b. 4
    c. 2
    d. 3

28. Simplify (3/5 - 2/5) + (3/4 – 2/8)

    a. 18/45
    b. 7/11
    c. 18/40
    d. 12/19

29. Solve for a. 6a + 4 = 28 + 2a

   a. 4
   b. 8
   c. 2
   d. 6

30. Simplify (3/4 - 1/4) - (3/5 – 2/5)

   a. 9/20
   b. 4/15
   c. 7/15
   d. 11/20

31. Solve for x. 6 + 9x = 12 + 7x

   a. 5
   b. 2
   c. 4
   d. 3

32. Simplify 6 2/5 / 2 2/7

   a. 2 1/4
   b. 1 1/5
   c. 2 4/5
   d. 2 2/3

33. Solve for a. -6 + 7a = 9 + 4a

   a. 3
   b. 5
   c. 2
   d. 6

34. A square lawn has an area of 62,500 square meters. What is the cost of building fence around it at a rate of $5.5 per meter?

    a. $4000
    b. $4500
    c. $5000
    d. $5500

35. The following numbers are the ages of people on a bus – 3, 6, 27, 13, 6, 8, 12, 20, 5, 10. Calculate their average of their ages.

    a. 11
    b. 6
    c. 9
    d. 110

36. A farmer wants to plant 65,536 trees in such a way that number of rows must be equal to the number of plants in a row. How many trees will he plant in a row?

    a. 1684
    b. 1268
    c. 668
    d. 256

37. How much pay does Mr. Johnson receive if he gives half of his pay to his family, $250 to his landlord, and has exactly 3/7 of his pay left after these expenses?

    a. $3600
    b. $3500
    c. $2800
    d. $1750

38. A boy has 4 red, 5 green and 2 yellow balls. He chooses two balls randomly. What is the probability that one is red and other is green?

    a. 2/11
    b. 19/22
    c. 20/121
    d. 9/11

39. Simplify 5 1/2 – 5 3/7

    a. 1/10
    b. 1/14
    c. 1/7
    d. 2/7

40. What is -3 - (-7) - (+5)?

    a. -6
    b. 6
    c. 3
    d. -1

41. Solve 3 3/4 x 4/5 x 1 3/4

    a. 3 3/4
    b. 4 1/3
    c. 6
    d. 5 1/4

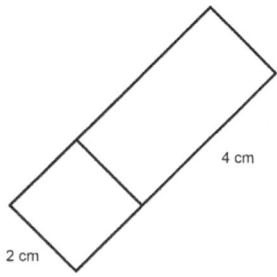

Note: figure not drawn to scale

42. Assuming the shape with a 2cm. side is square, what is the perimeter of the above shape?

    a. 12 cm
    b. 16 cm
    c. 6 cm
    d. 20 cm

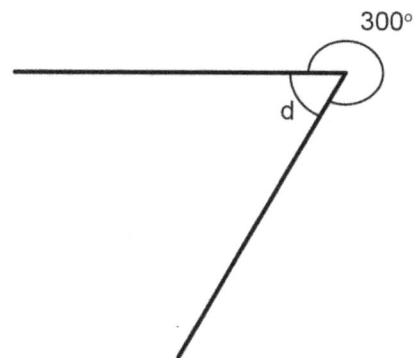

43. What is the measurement of the indicated angle?

    a. 45°
    b. 90°
    c. 60°
    d. 50°

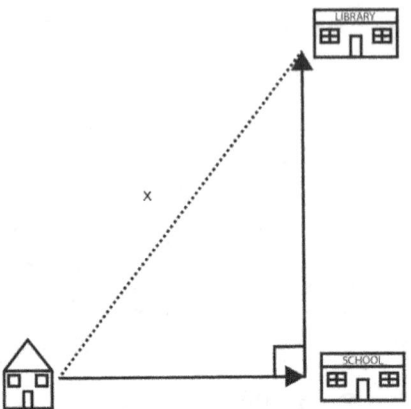

Note: figure not drawn to scale

44. Every day starting from his home Peter travels due east 3 kilometers to the school. After school he travels due north 4 kilometers to the library. What is the distance between Peter's home and the library?

    a. 15 km
    b. 10 km
    c. 5 km
    d. 12 ½ km

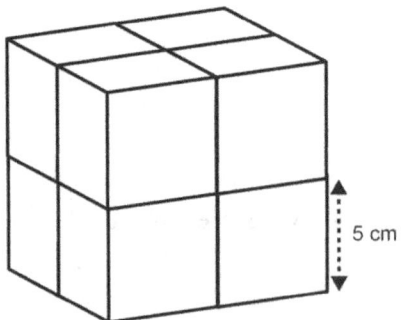

Note: figure not drawn to scale

45. What is the volume of the figure above?

    a. 125 cm³
    b. 875 cm³
    c. 1000 cm³
    d. 500 cm³

Answer Key

Section I Verbal Reasoning

1. B
Able and competent are synonyms.

2. A
Antidote and cure are synonyms.

3. C
Consensus and agreement are synonyms.

4. A
Magnify and amplify are synonyms.

5. B
Immaculate and perfect are synonyms.

6. C
Feasible and viable are synonyms.

7. B
Reason and rationale are synonyms.

8. A
Tinge and touch are synonyms.

9. C
Gist and summary are synonyms.

10. C
Initiate and instigate are synonyms.

11. A
Expertise and specialty are synonyms.

12. A
Fertile and fruitful are synonyms.

13. A
Rowdy and noisy are synonyms.

14. A
Courteous and polite are synonyms.

15. A
Lean and thin are synonyms.

16. B
Audacious and daring are synonyms.

17. A
Constitute and establish are synonyms.

18. A
Corrupt and unscrupulous are synonyms.

19. A
Dispense and distribute are synonyms.

20. B
Duration and length are synonyms.

21. B
Her talent was <u>extraordinary</u> (very unusual or remarkable) and so it wowed the audience.

22. C
Jean was <u>angry</u> when her little brother destroyed her favorite doll.

23. A
We will <u>ask</u> about our scores on the pop quiz.

24. A
The car accident was a <u>terrible</u> experience the victims want to forget.

25. C
Cinderella's <u>evil</u> (or commonly, wicked) stepmother failed in the end.

26. B
Her business success showed that she was very <u>astute</u> (having or showing an ability to accurately assess situations or people and turn this to one's advantage).

27. A
It is boring and I would rather not go, but the ceremony is <u>mandatory</u> (compulsory).

28. C
We don't want to hear the whole thing. Just the <u>relevant</u> (closely connected or appropriate to the matter at hand) facts please.

29. A
She works in a cubicle answering the phone all day. Her doctor says she is too <u>sedentary</u> (tending to spend much time seated; somewhat inactive).

30. B
I don't know why he is being so nice. I am sure he has an <u>ulterior</u> (beyond what is obvious or admitted) motive.

31. A
We cannot reveal the source. It was posted by <u>anonymous</u> (not identified by name; of unknown name).

32. C
I have never seen anyone so rude. His behavior was <u>atrocious</u> (wicked, horrifying)

33. B
I see that sign everywhere. It is much more <u>prevalent</u> (widespread) than I thought.

34. B
Her attitude was very <u>nonchalant</u> (casually calm and relaxed).

35. A
The water in the pond has been sitting for so long it is <u>stagnant</u> (lacking freshness, motion, flow, progress, or change; stale; motionless; still).

36. D
I cannot wait to try some of the <u>delicious</u> dishes served in the new restaurant.

37. B
Can you <u>describe</u> the character of Juliet in the play?

38. A
The soldiers <u>ruined</u> the rebel's camp. It is possible the soldiers could have fixed the rebel's camp, but generally soldiers and rebels are opposed, so 'ruined' is the best answer.

39. B
There is a big <u>dissimilarity</u> (difference) in Esther and Pete's grades. Since the comparison is between two students, choice B is the only one that makes sense.

40. D
I can <u>achieve</u> (attain) my goals in life when I study hard.

Section II – Quantitative Reasoning

1. A
(6 - 4) (3/5 – 4/5) = 2 (3 - 4/5) = since 3 is less than 4, we would have to subtract 1 from the whole number besides the fraction, therefore 1 13 - 4/5 = 1 9/5 = 2 4/5

2. B
46,227 + 101,032 = 147.259, or about 147,000.

3. A
$\sqrt{121} = 11$

4. B
Let the father's age = Y, and Kate's age = X, therefore Y = 32 + X, in 5 years y = 5x, substituting for Y will be 5x = 32 + X, 5x – x = 32, 4X = 32, X = 32/8, x = 8, Kate will be 8 in 5 years time, so Kate's present age = 8 - 5 = 3.

5. A
If she can type a full page in p minutes, then in 5 minutes she can type 5/p.

6. A
This is an inverse ratio problem.

1/x = 1/a + 1/b where a is the time Sally can paint a house, b is the time John can paint a house, x is the time Sally and John can together paint a house.

So,

1/x = 1/4 + 1/6 ... We use the least common multiple in the denominator that is 24:

1/x = 6/24 + 4/24

1/x = 10/24

x = 24/10

x = 2.4 hours.

In other words; 2 hours + 0.4 hours = 2 hours + 0.4•60 minutes

= 2 hours 24 minutes

7. B
Last season's ticket = X, 110%X = 880 tickets, %X = 880/110, 100%X = 880/110 x 100 = 800

8. B
This is an inverse proportion question. The number of employees decreases then working time will increase.

Employees   Working hours

12   7
10   x

Therefore, the equation will be
x/7 = 12/10
x = 7 * 12/10
x = 7.2

Therefore, the remaining staff will have to work, in minutes,

$0.2 \times 60 = 12$ minutes.

9. B
The speed is 300km/hr so it will cover 5 km/minute. Therefore, the train will travel 45km in 9 minutes. Time to arrive at station B will be 8:56 + 9 = 9:05 pm.

10. B
Suppose oranges in the basket before = x
Then according to the condition
$X + 8x/5 = 130$
$5x + 8x = 650$
$X = 50$

11. C
Number of problems remaining = 40 – 28 = 12
Time remaining = 30 – 25 = 5 minutes = 5 X 60 = 300 seconds. Time for each remaining question = 300/12 = 25 seconds.

12. B
$2/3Z + 10 = 3 \times 15$
$2/3 Z = 45 - 10$
$Z = 35 \times 3/2$
$Z = 52.5$

13. A
$1/3 \times 27 = 9 + 25 = 34$

14. A
The purchase price of 12 shirts when profit is 8% = 0.92 X 336 = $309. The purchase price of each shirt = 309/12 = $25.75

15. C
This is a proportionality question.
12 : 4
X : 20

4 * 5 = 20 and 12 * 5 = X
X = 60

16. C
Z = (5 X 5) – 10
Z = 15

17. A
2/3 of 100 = 66.66 X 5 = 333.33

18. B
.97 - .49 = .48
.76 + .21 = .97

19. B
1/3 + 1/5 + 3/6 = 10/30 + 6/30 + 15/30 = 31/30
2/3 + ¾ = 8/12 + 9/12 = 17/12

20. A
2/8 + 5/6 = 6/24 + 20/24 = 26/24
6/8 + 4/2 = 6/8 + 16/8 = 22/8

21. B
1800 X 16% = 288

22. A
The area of a square with 5 cm sides will be 5 X 5 = 25 cm2
The area of a rectangle with 2 cm and 10 cm sides will be 2 X 10 = 20 cm^2

23. A
Area of the circle = A = ∏ X r2   A = 3.14 X 192 = 1133.54
Area of the square = 25 X 25 = 625

24. A
Area of the circle = A = ∏ X r2   A = 3.14 X 92 = 254.34
Area of the triangle = ½ (B*H) = (5 X 10) / 2 = 25

25. A
40% of 500 = 200
12% of 1350 = 162

26. B
22% of 60 = 132
18% of 150 = 27

Practice Test Questions 2 — 161

27. B
15% of 50 = 7.5
12% of 75 = 9

28. A
.234 + .673 = .907
.990 - .378 = .612

29. A
Probability of drawing a red ball = 6/10
Probability of drawing a yellow ball = 4/10

30. A
Probability of drawing a red ball = 6/15
Probability of drawing a green ball = 4/15

31. B
75 X 22% = 16.5 so the cost is 75 − 16.5 = $58.50
100 X 35% = 35 so the cost is 100 − 35 = $65

32. B
.993 - .34 = .653
2/5 = .4

33. A
1/3 + 4/7 = 7/21 + 12/21 = 19/21 = .9047
6.93 - 6.34 = .59

34. A
.25 + .67 = 0.92
.89 - .34 = 0.55

35. A
.13 + .64 = .77
.62 - .14 = .48

Section III – Reading Comprehension

1. B
We can infer an important part of the respiratory system are the lungs. From the passage, "Molecules of oxygen and carbon dioxide are passively exchanged, by diffusion, be-

tween the gaseous external environment and the blood. This exchange process occurs in the alveolar region of the lungs."

Therefore, one primary function for the respiratory system is the exchange of oxygen and carbon dioxide, and this process occurs in the lungs. We can therefore infer that the lungs are an important part of the respiratory system.

2. C
The process by which molecules of oxygen and carbon dioxide are passively exchanged is diffusion.

This is a definition type question. Scan the passage for references to "oxygen," "carbon dioxide," or "exchanged."

3. A
The organ that plays an important role in gas exchange in amphibians is the skin.

Scan the passage for references to "amphibians," and find the answer.

4. A
The three physiological zones of the respiratory system are Conducting, transitional, respiratory zones.

5. B
This warranty does not cover a product that you have tried to fix yourself. From paragraph two, "This limited warranty does not cover ... any unauthorized disassembly, repair, or modification. "

6. C
ABC Electric could either replace or repair the fan, provided the other conditions are met. ABC Electric has the option to repair or replace.

7. B
The warranty does not cover a stove damaged in a flood. From the passage, "This limited warranty does not cover any damage to the product from improper installation, accident, abuse, misuse, natural disaster, insufficient or excessive electrical supply, abnormal mechanical or environmental conditions."

A flood is an "abnormal environmental condition," and a natural disaster, so it is not covered.

8. A
A missing part is an example of defective workmanship. This is an error made in the manufacturing process. A defective part is not considered workmanship.

9. B
The first paragraph tells us that myths are a true account of the remote past.

The second paragraph tells us that, "myths generally take place during a primordial age, when the world was still young, before achieving its current form."

Putting these two together, we can infer that humankind used myth to explain how the world was created.

10. A
This passage is about different types of stories. First, the passage explains myths, and then compares other types of stories to myths.

11. B
From the passage, "Unlike myths, folktales can take place at any time and any place, and the natives do not usually consider them true or sacred."

12. A
Based on the partial table of contents, this book is most likely about how to answer multiple choice.

13. B
This passage describes the different categories for traditional stories. The other options are facts from the passage, not the main idea of the passage. The main idea of a passage will always be the most general statement. For example, choice A, Myths, fables, and folktales are not the same thing, and each describes a specific type of story. This is a true statement from the passage, but not the main idea of the passage, since the passage also talks about how some cultures may classify a story as a myth and others as a folktale.

The statement, from choice B, Traditional stories can be

categorized in different ways by different people, is a more general statement that describes the passage.

14. B
Choice B is the best choice, categories that group traditional stories according to certain characteristics.

Choices A and C are false and can be eliminated right away. Choice D is designed to confuse. Choice D may be true, but it is not mentioned in the passage.

15. D
The best answer is choice D, traditional stories themselves are a part of the larger category of folklore, which may also include costumes, gestures, and music.

All the other choices are false. Traditional stories are part of the larger category of Folklore, which includes other things, not the other way around.

16. A
There is a distinct difference between a myth and a legend, although both are folktales.

17. A
Choice A is a re-wording of text from the passage.

18. C
This is taken directly from the passage.

19. C
Although trees are used as a building material, this is not their primary use. Trees are a primary energy source.

20. A
This is taken directly from the passage.

21. D
This question is designed to confuse by presenting different choices for the two chemicals, oxygen and carbon dioxide. One is produced, and one is reduced. Read the passage carefully to see which is reduced and which is produced.

22. D
This question tests the reader's summarization skills. The other answers A, B, and C focus on portions of the second

paragraph that are too narrow and do not relate to the specific portion of text in question. The complexity of the sentence may mislead students into selecting one of these answers, but rearranging or restating the sentence will lead the reader to the correct answer. In addition, A makes an assumption that may or may not be true about the intentions of the company, B focuses on one product rather than the idea of the products, and C makes an assumption about women that may or may not be true and is not supported by the text.

23. B
This question tests reader's attention to detail. If a reader selects A, he or she may have picked up on the use of the word "debate" and assumed, very logically, that the two are at odds because they are fighting; however, this is simply not supported in the text. C also uses very specific quotes from the text, but it rearranges them and gives them false meaning. The artists want to elevate their creations above the creations of other artists, thereby showing that they are "creative" and "innovative." Similarly, D takes phrases straight from the texts and rearranges and confuses them. The artists are described as wanting to be "creative, innovative, individual people," not the women.

24. A
This question tests reader's vocabulary and summarization skills. This phrase, used by the author, may seem flippant and dismissive if readers focus on the word "whatever" and misinterpret it as a popular, colloquial terms. In this way, the answers B and C may mislead the reader to selecting one of them by including the terms "unimportant" and "stupid," respectively. D is a similar misreading, but doesn't make sense when the phrase is at the beginning of the passage and the entire passage is on media messages. A is literarily and contextually appropriate, and the reader can understand that the author would like to keep the introduction focused on the topic the passage is going to discuss.

25. A
This question tests a reader's inference skills. The extreme use of the word "all" in B suggests that every single advertising company are working to be approachable, and while this is not only unlikely, the text specifically states that "more"

companies have done this, signifying that they have not all participated, even if it's a possibility that they may some day. The use of the limiting word "only" in C lends that answer similar problems; women are still buying from companies who do not care about this message, or those companies would not be in business, and the passage specifies that "many" women are worried about media messages, but not all. Readers may find D logical, especially if they are looking to make an inference, and while this may be a possibility, the passage does not suggest or discuss this happening. A is correct based on specifically because of the relation between "still working" in the answer and "will hopefully" and the extensive discussion on companies struggles, which come only with progress, in the text.

26. B
The time limit for radar detectors is 14 days. Since you made the purchase 15 days ago, you do not qualify for the guarantee.

27. B
Since you made the purchase 10 days ago, you are covered by the guarantee. Since it is an advertised price at a different store, ABC Electric will "beat" the price by 10% of the difference, which is,

500 – 400 = 100 – difference in price

100 X 10% = $10 – 10% of the difference

The advertised lower price is $400. ABC will beat this price by 10% so they will refund $100 + 10 = $110.

28. C
The purpose of this passage is to persuade.

29. B
From the first paragraph, "The segments of the body are organized into three distinctive connected units, a head, a thorax, and an abdomen."
This question tries to confuse 'segments' and 'units.'

30. D
This question tries to confuse. Read the passage carefully

to find reference to the number of wings. "...if present in the species, two or four wings."

From this, we can conclude some insects have no wings, (if present ...) some have 2 wings and some have 4 wings.

31. A
The question asks about the abdomen and choices refer to organs in the abdomen. The passage says, "The abdomen also contains most of the digestive, respiratory, ... "

The choices are,

      a. It contains some of the organs.

      b. It is too small for any organs.

      c. It contains all of the organs.

      d. None of the above.

Choice A is true, but we need to see if there is better choice before answering. Choice B is not true. Choice C is not true since the relevant sentence says 'most' not 'all.' Choice D can be eliminated since Choice A is true.

Given there is not better choice, Choice A is the best choice answer.

32. A
This best summary statement of this passage is, this passage is about the physical characteristics of insects.

33. A
We can infer that an important purpose of the circulatory system is that of fighting diseases.

34. B
Humans have a closed circulatory system.

35. C
Besides blood, the heart and the blood vessels form the cardiovascular system.

36. B
The digestive system, along with the circulatory system, helps provide nutrients to keep the human heart pumping.

37. C
This question tests the reader's summarization skills. The entire passage is leading up to the idea that the president of the US may not have had grounds to assert his Fourteen Points when other countries had lost so much. A is pretty directly inferred by the text, but it does not adequately summarize what the entire passage is trying to communicate. B may also be inferred by the passage when it says that the war is "imminent," but it does not represent the entire message, either. The passage does seem to be in praise of FDR, or at least in respect of him, but it does not in any way claim that he is the smartest president, nor does this represent the many other points included. C is then the obvious answer, and most directly relates to the closing sentences which it rewords.

38. C
This question tests the reader's attention to detail. The passage does state that A and B are true, and while those statements are in proximity to the explanation for why the war started, they are not the actual reason given. D is a mix up of words used in the passage, which says that the largest powers were in play but not that this fact somehow started the war. The passage does make a direct statement that a domino effect started the war, supporting C as the correct answer.

39. A
This question tests the reader's understanding of functions in writing. Throughout the passage, it states that leaders of other nations were hesitant to accept generous or peaceful terms because of the grievances of the war, and the great loss of life was chief among these. While the passage does touch on the devastation of deadly weapons (B), the use of this raw, emotional fact serves a much larger purpose, and the focus of the passage is not the weapons. While readers may indeed consider who lost the most soldiers (C) when many countries were involved and the inequalities of loss are mentioned in the passage, there is no discussion of this in the passage. D is related to A, But A is more direct and relates more to the passage.

40. B
This question tests the reader's vocabulary skills. A may seem appealing to readers because it is phonetically similar to "catalyzed," but the two are not related in any other way. C makes sense in context, but if plugged in to the sentence creates a redundancy that doesn't make sense. D does also not make sense contextually, even if the reader may consider that funds were needed to create more weaponry, especially if it was advanced.

Section V – Math

1. B
Let XY represent the initial number, X + Y = 12, YX=XY+ 36, only b = 48 satisfies both equations.

2. A
The problem is to find the perimeter of a shape made by merging a square and a semi circle. Perimeter = 3 sides of the square + 1/2 circumference of the circle.
= (3 x 5) + ½(5 π)
= 15 + 2.5 π
Perimeter = 17.5 π cm

3. B
Volume = Volume of large cylinder - Volume of small cylinder (Volume of cylinder = area of base x height)
Volume = (π 12^2 x 10) - (π 6^2 x 5), 1440π - 180π
Volume = 1260π in^3

4. D
We have a circle given with diameter 8 cm and a square located within the circle. We are asked to find the area of the circle for which we only need to know the length of the radius that is the half of the diameter.

Area of circle = πr^2 ... r = 8/2 = 4 cm

Area of circle = π•4^2

= 16π cm^2 ... As we notice, the inner square has no role in this question.

5. C
In one trip around the track, he covers the distance equal to the circumference of the circular path.
Circumference of the path = 75 × π = 235.65 meters.
Distance covered in 7 times around = 235.65 × 7 = 1650 meters.

6. A
The angles opposite both angles 30° & angle d are respectively equal to vertical angles.
2(30° + d) = 360°
2d = 360° - 60°
2d = 300°
d = 150°

7. C
The length of the track = 1.2 km = 1200 meters.
John will complete 1 round in 1200/120 = 10 minutes.
Tony will complete 1 round in 1200/100 = 12 minutes.
David will complete 1 round in 1200/75 = 16 minutes.
The Least Common Multiple of these is 240. Therefore, they will be together after 240 minutes.

8. D
1 cm = 5 km so 12.4 cm will be = 12.4 × 5 = 62 km.

9. B
Perimeter of a parallelogram is the sum of the sides.

Perimeter = 2(l+b)
Perimeter = 2(3+10), 2 x 13
Perimeter = 26 cm

10. D
2009 X 108 is approximately 210,000. The actual number is 216,972.

11. D
First, convert everything to seconds.
Song A = 240 + 56 = 296 sec.
Song B = 120 + 30 = 150 sec.
Song C = 600 + 16 = 616 sec.
Total = 296 + 150 + 616 = 1062. Average will be 1062/3 =

354.
In hours, 354/60 = 5 minutes, 54 seconds.

12. B
8.50 * .4 = 3.40 + 1.30 = $4.70

13. B
Formula for perimeter of a rectangle is 2(L + W)
p=26, so 2(L+W) = p

The length is 5 inches more than the width, so
2(w+5) + 2w = 26
2w + 10 + 2w = 26
2w + 2w = 26 - 10
4w = 18
W = 16/4 = 4 inches
L is 5 inches more than w, so
L = 5 + 4 = 9 inches.

14. D
Substitute the known variables, (3 x 2) + (4 x 4) x 8 =, 6 + 16 x 8, 24 x 8 = 176

15. A
2cnx = 2(4 x 5 x 3)/(2 X 5) =
(2 x 60)/(2 x 5) = 120/10 = 12

16. A
First change all the terms to fractions, therefore, we get 7/2 / 14/5, to divide we need to invert the second fraction, 7/2 x 5/14, and then we cancel out to reduce to the lowest terms, 1/2 x 5/2 = 5/4, convert back to proper fraction to get 1 1/4

17. B
Substitute known variables, 2 x 9/3 + 3 x 10/5 – 2 =, 18/3 + 30/5 – 2 =, 6 + 6 -2 =, 12 - 2 = 10

18. A
First solve the fraction in each bracket separately, therefore (1/3 + 2/6) - (3/4 - 1/3) = (find common denominator) (2+2/6) – (9- 4/12) = (4/6) – (5/12) = (find common denominator again) 2/3 – 5/12 =, 8 - 5/12 = 3/12 = 1/4.

19. B
(4/5 - 3/10) + (2/3 – 3/9) =, (find a common denominator)
(8-3/10) + (6-3/9) =, (5/10) + (3/9) = 2/5 + 1/3, (find a common denominator) 6+5/15 = 11/15

20. A
2 + a number divided by 7.
(2 + X) divided by 7.
(2 + X)/7

21. D
Substitute with known variables, (6 x 8) – 12 + (2 x 12) =,
48 – 12 + 24, do the additions first, 48 – (12 + 24) =, 48 – 36 = 12

22. C
Subtract the whole numbers and then subtract the fractions, therefore 3 2/3 - 1 2/8 = (3-1) (2/3 – 2/8) = find common denominator to subtract the fractions, (2) (16-6)/24 = 2 10/24, reduce to lowest terms, 2 5/12

23. A
Subtract the whole numbers and then subtract the fractions, therefore (7-4) (2/5 – 3/10) = 3 (4-3/10) = 3 1/10

24. C
-4 – 5x = 8x + 8, bring same terms to same side of the equation changing the negative or positive signs when they cross over, therefore -5x +8x = 8 + 4, = 3x = 12, x = 12/3 = 4.

25. A
First, convert all the terms to fractions and then cancel out. Therefore, 7/3 x 10/7 x 3/4 = 1/3 x 10/1 x 3/4, 1 x 5 x 1/2, 5 x 1/2 = 2 1/2

26. B
Subtract the whole numbers and then subtract the fractions, therefore (7 - 4) (4/5 – 2/3) = 3 (12 - 10/15) =
3 2/15

27. C
12x – 8 = 3x + 10, bring same terms to same side of the equation changing the negative or positive signs when they

cross over, therefore 12x -3x = 10 + 8, 9x = 18, x = 2

28. C
(3/5 - 2/5) + (3/4 – 2/8) =, (3-2/5) + (6 - 2/8) =, 1/5 + 4/8 =, (find a common denominator) 8+10/40 = 18/40

29. D
6a + 4 = 28 + 2a, solve for a. Bring same terms to same side of the equation changing the negative or positive signs when they cross over, therefore 6a – 2a = 28 - 4, 4a = 24, a = 24/4 = 6

30. D
(3-1/4) – (3-2/5) =, 3/4 - 1/5 =. 15-4/20 = 11/20

31. D
6 + 9x = 12 + 7x, bring same terms to same side of the equation changing the negative or positive signs when they cross over, therefore 9x – 7x = 12 – 6, 2x = 6, x = 6/2, x = 3

32. C
First change all the terms to fractions, therefore, we get 32/5 / 16/7, to divide we need to invert the second fraction, 32/5 x 7/16, and then we cancel out to reduce to the lowest terms, 2/5 x 7/1 = 14/5, convert back to proper fraction to get 2 4/5

33. B
-6 + 7a = 9 + 4a, bring same terms to same side of the equation changing the negative or positive signs when they cross over, therefore 7a – 4a = 9 + 6 = 3a = 15, a = 15/3, a = 5

34. D
As the lawn is square, the length of one side will be= $\sqrt{62500}$ = 250 meters. Therefore, the perimeters will be 250 × 4 = 1000 meters. The total cost will be 1000 × 5.5 = $5500.

35. A
First add all the numbers 3 + 6 + 27 + 13 + 6 + 8 + 12 + 20 + 5 + 10 = 110. Then divide by 10 (the number of data provided) = 110/10 = 11

36. D
Let x be number of rows, and number of trees in a row. So equation becomes X^2 = 65536, X = 256.

37. B
We check the fractions in the question and see that there is a "half" (that is 1/2) and 3/7. So, we multiply the denominators of these fractions to decide how to name the total money. We say that Mr. Johnson has 14x at the beginning; he gives half of this, meaning 7x, to his family. $250 to his landlord. He has 3/7 of his money left. 3/7 of 14x is equal to:

14x•(3/7) = 6x

So,

Spent money is: 7x + 250

Unspent money is: 6x

Total money is: 14x

We write an equation: total money = spent money + unspent money

14x = 7x + 250 + 6x

14x - 7x - 6x = 250

x = 250

We are asked to find the total money that is 14x:

14x = 14•250 = $3500

38. A
The probability that the 1st ball drawn is red = 4/11. The probability that the 2nd ball drawn is green = 5/10. The combined probability will then be 4/11 X 5/10 = 20/110 = 2/11.

39. B
(5-5) (1/2 − 3/7) = (7-6/14) = 1/14

40. D
-(-) becomes + and -(+) becomes -, therefore, -3 - (-7) - (+5) = -3 + 7 − 5, -4 + 5 = -1

41. D
First, convert all the terms to fractions and then cancel out. Therefore, 15/4 x 4/5 x 7/4 = 3/4 x 4/1 x 7/4, 3/4 x 1/1 x 7/1, 21/4 = 5 1/4

42. B
We see that there is a square with side 2 cm and a rectangle adjacent to it, with one side 2 cm (common side with the square) and the other side 4 cm. The perimeter of a shape is found by summing up all sides surrounding the shape, not adding the ones inside the shape. Three 2 cm sides from the square, and two 4 cm sides and one 2 cm side from the rectangle contribute the perimeter.

So, the perimeter of the shape is: 2 + 2 + 2 + 4 + 2 + 4 = 16 cm.

43. C
The sum of angles around a point is 360°
d + 300 = 360°
d = 60°

44. C
Pythagorean Theorem:
$(Hypotenuse)^2 = (Perpendicular)^2 + (Base)^2$
$h^2 = a^2 + b^2$

Given: $3^2 + 4^2 = h^2$
$h^2 = 9 + 16$
$h = \sqrt{25}$
h = 5

45. C
Large cube is made up of 8 smaller cubes of 5 cm sides.
Volume = Volume of small cube x 8
Volume = (5 x 5 x 5) x 8, 125 x 8
Volume = 1000 cm^3

Conclusion

CONGRATULATIONS! You have made it this far because you have applied yourself diligently to practicing for the exam and no doubt improved your potential score considerably! Getting into a good school is a huge step in a journey that might be challenging at times but will be many times more rewarding and fulfilling. That is why being prepared is so important.

Good Luck!

FREE Ebook Version

Download a FREE Ebook version of the publication!

Suitable for tablets, iPad, iPhone, or any smart phone.

Go to
http://tinyurl.com/khysnhe

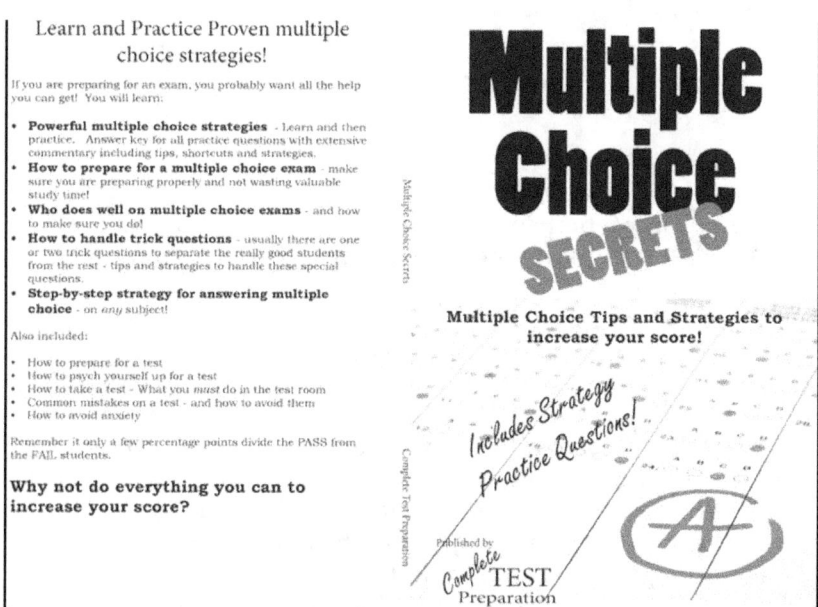

Learn to increase your score using time-tested secrets for answering multiple choice questions!

This practice book has everything you need to know about answering multiple choice questions on a standardized test!

You will learn 12 strategies for answering multiple choice questions and then practice each strategy with over 45 reading comprehension multiple choice questions, with extensive commentary from exam experts!

Maybe you have read this kind of thing before, and maybe feel you don't need it, and you are not sure if you are going to buy this Book.

Remember though, it only a few percentage points divide the PASS from the FAIL students.

Even if our multiple choice strategies increase your score by a few percentage points, isn't that worth it?

www.multiple-choice.ca

Endnotes

Reading Comprehension passages where noted below are used under the Creative Commons Attribution-ShareAlike 3.0 License

http://en.wikipedia.org/wiki/Wikipedia:Text_of_Creative_Commons_Attribution-ShareAlike_3.0_Unported_License

[1] Virus. In *Wikipedia*. Retrieved November 12, 2010 from http://en.wikipedia.org/wiki/Virus.
[2] Thunderstorm. In *Wikipedia*. Retrieved November 12, 2010 from en.wikipedia.org/wiki/Thunderstorm.
[3] Meteorology. In *Wikipedia*. Retrieved November 12, 2010 from en.wikipedia.org/wiki/Outline_of_meteorology.
[4] Cloud. In *Wikipedia*. Retrieved November 12, 2010 from http://en.wikipedia.org/wiki/Clouds.
[5] U.S. Navy Seal. In *Wikipedia*. Retrieved November 12, 2010 from en.wikipedia.org/wiki/United_States_Navy_SEALs.
[6] Gardens. In *Wikipedia*. Retrieved November 12, 2010 from en.wikipedia.org/wiki/Gardens.
[7] Mythology. In *Wikipedia*. Retrieved November 12, 2010 from en.wikipedia.org/wiki/Mythology.
[8] Tree. In *Wikipedia*. Retrieved November 12, 2010 from en.wikipedia.org/wiki/tree.
[9] Insect. In *Wikipedia*. Retrieved November 12, 2010 from en.wikipedia.org/wiki/Insect.
[10] Circulatory System. In Wikipedia. Retrieved November 12,2010 from http://en.wikipedia.org/wiki/Circulatory_System.

www.ingramcontent.com/pod-product-compliance
Lightning Source LLC
Chambersburg PA
CBHW070859080526
44589CB00013B/1129